Fallen Angels, Watchers, Giants, Nephilim and Evil

Fallen Angels, Watchers, Giants, Nephilim and Evil.
©Translation and notes by Dr A. Nyland.
© Copyright by Dr A. Nyland 2011.
First edition
All rights reserved.
ISBN 9781461168362
All rights reserved under International Copyright Law.
All Hebrew Bible and New Testament Scripture taken from *The Source Bible* ©.
No part of this book may be stored or reproduced in any form without the express written permission of the copyright holder. Permission queries to *horsecare (at) y7mail (dot) com*. *The Source* translation may be quoted in any form (written, electronic, audio, visual) up to and inclusive of 500 (five hundred) verses for non-commercial purposes without express written permission of the copyright holder, providing that the verses quoted do not compromise 25% or more of the total text of the work or do not amount to a complete book of the Bible in the work in which they are quoted.
The notes may not be copied under any circumstances.
Notice of copyright must appear on the title or copyright page of the work as follows: Scripture taken from *The Source Bible*. Copyright © 2010 by Dr A. Nyland. Used by permission. All rights reserved.
It is not necessary to use the complete notice of copyright in non-saleable media, such as church newsletters, church bulletins, church handouts, orders of service, posters, transparencies, but the words "The Source Bible" must appear at the end of each quotation.

www.dranyland.blogspot.com

Cover illustration by Robyn Montrec.
www.montrecart.blogspot.com

Contents

1. Introduction.   5
2. Mistakes about Fallen Angels and Nephilim   9
3. Watchers.   13
4. Punishment of the Watchers.   37
5. Individual Fallen Angels.   43
6. The Watchers who did not Fall.   55
7. Nephilim and Giants.   65
8. Origins of Evil.   81
9. Was Satan a Fallen Angel?   89
Endnotes   93

Chapter 1. Introduction.

Watchers were a class of angel. Some of the Watchers came to earth and taught weapons, spell potions, root cuttings, astrology, astronomy and alchemies to the humans living on earth. Some of the Watchers slept with human women. Nephilim were the progeny of the Watchers and the human women. The word "Nephilim" is translated as "Giants" in certain older Bible versions. This can be misleading, as the term "Giants" in those days referred to a class of non-human entities and not just to tall people or to figures like the Giant in the fairytale *Jack and the Beanstalk*. Word meaning often changes over centuries.

For this act, the Watchers were punished by being bound and cast into Tartarus. This is stated explicitly in the Hebrew Bible / Old Testament and New Testament as well as in other ancient literature. It was a common belief of the times. The Hebrew Bible / Old Testament and New Testament (in original languages, as this has been widely mistranslated into English) also explicitly blame the acts of the Watchers for the flood, and for the destruction of Sodom.

Interestingly, Greek mythology speaks of *gigantes* being thrown into Tartarus. *Gigantes* is the word which the *Septuagint* uses to translate the Hebrew word "Nephilim." The texts of the Hebrew Bible, referred to by Christians as the Old Testament (although "Old Covenant" is the proper translation) are the Masoretic Text and the *Septuagint*. The Masoretic Text is Hebrew, and named after the Masoretes, the schools of scribes and Torah scholars who copied and edited the text between the 7th and 10th centuries AD. The oldest copies of the Masoretic Text we have today date to the 9th century AD.

The *Septuagint* (often written "LXX"), the ancient Greek text from the period of the 3rd to 2nd centuries BCE, is translated from the Hebrew texts of the times. The *Septuagint* is quoted in the New Testament. It was widely used by the Hellenistic Jews of the time.

The Watchers who slept with the human women and taught the humans are referred to these days as "Fallen Angels." However, not all the Watchers disobeyed by having sex with human women and by teaching humans, only certain Watchers. Thus not all Watchers are Fallen Angels, but the Fallen Angels mentioned by Enoch did come from the class of angel known as Watchers.

1 Enoch 6 states, "When the angels,[1] the inhabitants of heaven, saw them (*the human women*), they lusted after them and said to each other, 'Come on, let's choose consorts for ourselves from the humans, and let's produce children!'"

Angels are actually "messengers." The word for "angel" in Greek and Hebrew was the same word for a human messenger. There was not a separate word for the heavenly beings.[2] The English word "angel" is a transliteration of the Greek word, and not a translation. To "transliterate" (noun, "transliteration") means to put letters from a language whose letters are nothing like English letters, into English letters. "Angels" is the transliteration but the meaning is "messengers." The Hebrew word for "angel" actually means one dispatched as a deputy.

The ancient *Books of Enoch* are the best sources for the Fallen Angels, Watchers and Nephilim. There are three *Books of Enoch*, all of which are unrelated to the other. The book which was known for centuries as the "*Book of Enoch*" is usually now called *1 Enoch* to distinguish it from the later *The Secrets of Enoch*, also known as *2 Enoch*. Many ancient sources referred to the *Book of Enoch*, but it was not until 1773 that James Bruce discovered three copies in Ethiopia. *1 Enoch* is also called the *Ethiopic Enoch*, and *2 Enoch* is also known as *Slavonic Enoch*. The *Third Book of Enoch* is also known as the *Hebrew Book of Enoch*, as the evidence suggests it was originally written in Hebrew.

The *Book of Enoch* (1 Enoch) was left out of the Canon, but a lengthy passage from the *Book of Enoch* is quoted by Jude. This cast doubts upon Jude's inclusion in the New Testament canon. The early church father Tertullian considered that the *Book of Enoch* should be included in the canon. The third century Bible translator (into Latin) Jerome stated, "Jude, James' brother, left a short letter which is considered among the seven broad letters, and because in it he quotes from the apocryphal book of Enoch it is rejected by many.

Nonetheless by age and use it has gained authority and is considered among the Holy Scriptures."[3]

The authorship of *1 Enoch* is contentious, but there is general agreement that several authors contributed to what we now call the *Book of Enoch*. Enoch was the son of Jared, great grandfather of Noah, and father of Methuselah, not to be confused with the Enoch who was the eldest son of Cain.

Chapter 2. Mistakes about Fallen Angels and Nephilim.

Before we examine the accounts of the Watchers in ancient sources, I will mention the English mistranslations which can lead to confusion, namely the so-called "Sons of God" and "Daughters of men."

The phrase often mistranslated into English as "sons of men," "children of men," actually meant "people," "humans." The Hebrew or Greek word "children/sons" with a noun refers to a member of a class of people, and should not be translated as "son/child of." The phrase "sons of (place name)" /"children of (place name)" again refers to inhabitants of that place. The *Benai Israel*, (mis)translated in the King James Version as "children/sons of Israel" actually means "members of the class of people called Israel" and should be translated as "Israelites." The expression is also Greek, and found as early as Homer. The same is the case in the New Testament, where the Greek word *huios* is placed with the word "Israel," and should be translated as "Israelites" rather than translated as "children of Israel" or "sons of Israel" which is a translation error.

The word *huios* is often used with a noun to express a similarity with the noun. For example, an ancient Greek would put the word *huios* (son, child) with a word meaning "loud" to mean "the loud one" or to refer to a person who shouts frequently. In word-for-word Greek, the same expression would appear as "child/son of loudness," but such a (mis)translation is not the correct meaning.

In Aristophanes' (the famous comic playwright of the fifth century B.C.) play *Acharnians*, 1150, *Antimachon ton Psakados* appears to be word-for-word "Antimachos child/son of showers" but proper translation method demands we translate as "Antimachos the spitter" or similar. The Scholiast states that he was so-named because he spat when speaking and "showered spray on those who were talking to him."

The King James Version thought the Hebrew expression "hostile people" meant "sons of Hostility" and that "Hostility" was a pagan god. That is why all other Bible versions[4] have translated this expression as "hostile people" while the King James Version has "sons of Belial." It is a simple but serious translation error.

In the same way, "sons of God" is a mistranslation for "associates of God,"[5] and "daughters of men" is a mistranslation for "human women." This misunderstanding of basic translation principles led Saint Augustine, the Catholic Bishop of Hippo, among others, to state that "sons of God" referred to the genealogical line of Seth. Augustine wrote that Genesis 6 meant that the male descendents of Adam through Seth were "the sons of God," and the female descendents of Adam through Cain were "the daughters of men."[6]

The phrase "Son of Man" is a mistranslation and this mistranslation has led to non-scholars jumping to wrongful conclusions.

The ancient Greek expression *ho huios tou anthropou* means a person associated with humanity. It is a translation of *bar nasha,* an Aramaic periphrasis for "person," and would be read word for word as "one associated with humanity" as it is in non-gender specific language and "humanity" is in the singular. However, *bar nasha* means "one associated with people," "a person," "the person," "humanity," "the representative person." The Anchor Bible translates "The Man." The title is a direct reference to Daniel 7:13-14.[7]

Bear in mind that the range of meanings possessed by a word is called its "semantic range." Not all those meanings relate to each other. Here is the semantic range of the English word "port:" a suitcase, a strong wine, a harbor, the left side of the ship. Note that the word "port" does not have all these meanings at the same time. Here I have just used the expression "bear in mind." In this expression, the word "bear" does not mean a wild animal that would chase me and eat me. In the same way too, *bar nasha* has several different meanings. This is the normal way that language works.

Some commentaries have made erroneous statements about "Son of Man" based on the exegetical fallacy termed "illegitimate totality transfer," that is, supposing that the meaning of a word in a one particular context expands to others in its semantic range in conflict with its context.

Despite some wild claims on the internet, the *Book of Jasher* does not mention Nephilim or Fallen Angels at all. The following passage some have tried to connect with the Fallen Angels, but it only mentions humans.

11 Lamech was 180 years old when he married Ashmua, the daughter of Elishaa the son of his uncle Enoch his uncle, and she conceived.

12 And at that time the humans sowed the ground, yet produced little food. However, the humans did not turn from their evil ways, and sinned and rebelled against God.

13 Lamech's wife conceived and gave birth to a son at that time, at the revolution of the year.

14 Methuselah called him Noah, and said, "In his time the earth was at rest and corruption free," and Lamech his father called him Menachem, and said, "This one will comfort us in our actions and miserable labor in the earth, which God has cursed."

15 The child grew up and was weaned, and he acted like his ancestor Methuselah, completely upright with God.

16 All the humans left the Lord's ways in those times as their numbers increased on the earth, having with sons and daughters. They taught one another their evil practices and they kept sinning against the Lord.

17 Every one made a god for themselves, and everyone robbed and plundered their neighbors and relatives. They made the earth corrupt, and the earth was filled with violence.

18 Their judges and rulers went to the human women and forcefully took women they chose from their husbands. In those days the humans took the cattle of the earth, the wild animals of the field and the birds of the air, and taught the interbreeding of one species with the other, in order to provoke the Lord.[8]

Verse 18 is the passage which some have alleged is connected with Fallen Angels, although the verse mentions only humans. Interbreeding of species was against the Law of Moses. Ritually unclean acts mentioned in Leviticus 18 include wearing clothing made of two different types of material, planting two different types of crops in the same field and breeding two different types of cattle together.

In an apparent confusion of Hebrew verbs, popular author Zecharia Sitchin claims that the Nephilim were those who came down from above, those who were cast down, and people of the fiery rockets. Sitchin also identifies the Nephilim with the Sumerian deities, claiming that the Sumerians knew of their existence and that they came from a planet called Nibiru. I am not saying this is correct or incorrect; I am simply stating that Sitchin's comment on the meaning of the word "Nephilim" is invalid.

In the second century CE, Rabbi Simeon ben Yochai pronounced a curse on any Jews who believed that the angels were fathers of the Nephilim. Rabbi Moshe ben Nachman (Nachmanides) and Rabbi Shlomo Yitzchaki (Rashi) followed this viewpoint.

Chapter 3. Watchers.

First of all, it is important to note that the ancient Greek word for "Watchers" is "Grigori." Watchers and Grigori are one and the same. Some angel books are under the misapprehension that they are different classes of angels, but they were not. "Grigori" simply means "Watchers" in ancient Greek.

As mentioned in the previous chapter, the First Book of Enoch contains accounts of the Watchers, a class of angel. Not all the Watchers disobeyed by teaching humans and having sex with human women.

The Hebrew Bible/Old Testament mentions a Watcher in Daniel 4:13 and 4:17: "a sacred Watcher came down from heaven." Here the word translated "Watcher" is Aramaic. The expression appears to be "a watcher and a sacred/holy one" but this is a grammatical point called *hendiadys*, where (for example) the word "and" is put between two nouns but the expression should be read as one the nouns being an adjective. Thus this expression here in English is "a sacred Watcher."

Nebuchadnezzar tells Daniel that he saw in a vision or dream a "sacred Watcher" who appeared to him and made an announcement.

"While I was in my bed I had a vision in my head in which a sacred Watcher came down out of heaven. He loudly called out the following. 'Chop down the tree and lop off its branches! Strip off its foliage and disperse its fruit! Let the animals flee from under it and the birds from its branches, but leave its main root in the ground. Put a band of iron and bronze around it, in the grass of the field. Let it become damp with the dew of the sky, and let its fate be to live with the animals in the grass of the ground.

"'Let his mind be changed from a human being's mind, and let an animal's mind be given to him, and let this happen to him for seven periods of time.

"'This announcement is by the decree of the Watchers; this command is by the word of the sacred ones, so that those who are alive may understand that the Supreme has authority over the human kingdoms, and he gives it to whomever he wishes. He sets up even the lowest ranked human beings over them." (Daniel 4:13-18 from *The Source*.)

Next we will examine the account in *The Book of Jubilees*. *The Book of Jubilees* is sometimes called *Little (Lesser) Genesis*, the *Testament of Moses*, or the *Apocalypse of Moses*. There is general scholarly agreement that *The Book of Jubilees* dates from 160-150 BCE.

The *Book of Jubilees* contains information additional to Genesis and early Exodus, and is the account from creation to the early times of Moses.

Jubilees are seven "year-weeks," a year-week being a period of seven years, so a jubilee is 49 years. The chronology is based on multiples of seven.

The *Book of Jubilees* claims to be told to Moses by angels when he was on Mount Sinai. Translator R.H. Charles stated that the author of Jubilees was a Pharisee,[9] but later commentators have rightly pointed out that this is untenable.

There are twenty seven Ethiopic texts of *The Book of Jubilees*, and manuscripts in Greek, a Latin translation of the Greek, and Syriac. Fifteen Jubilees scrolls written in Hebrew were discovered at Qumran between 1947 and 1956. Scholars have suggested it was originally written in Hebrew, and presents a separate source to the Masoretic text and the *Septuagint* (or Hebrew original of the *Septuagint*).

The Book of Jubilees is divided into fifty chapters, and appears to be complete. It is clear that the author of Jubilees has knowledge of 1 Enoch.

The *Book of Jubilees* is considered canon by the Ethiopian Orthodox Church. However, most Catholic, Protestant and Eastern orthodox churches consider it pseudegraphical.

One of the Dead Sea Scrolls, *The Damascus Document,* states that the *Book of Jubilees* reveals divine secrets "to which Israel has turned a blind eye."[10] The Essenes, a Jewish sect who lived from the 2nd century BCE to the 1st century ACE, coveted the *Book of Jubilees* and kept it in their library.[11] Josephus and Philo note that the Essenes "practiced strict celibacy" and that the war in which the Essenes saw themselves engaged was God's battle against the power of a spiritual war.[12] The Essenes turned all money and property over to their leaders and lived without money.[13] Philo states that the Essene community grew to over 4,000 men.[14] Women appear to have been subordinate. The Essenes had no part in secular life and lived a monastic life in caves overlooking the Dead Sea.[15] They dressed only in white and the priestly leaders strictly interpreted the law for them.[16] The Essenes saw things as black and white. They considered themselves to be God's people and considered that everyone else belonged to the evil one.

The Essene movement was exclusive and restricted to freeborn male Jews, and also to the select few who were willing to join them. The Essenes called themselves the "associates of light" and labeled others the "associates of darkness," "assembly of traitors," and "(people who) depart from the way, have contravened the law, and violated the precept."[17]

The Essenes believed that the sins of the people wiped out the Abrahamic covenant, and that people must now join the new covenant of their assembly.[18] A man who wanted to join the desert community must confess himself to be free of sin. The man is under probation for several years. He must hand over his property to the community leaders and swear to practice sexual abstinence and to follow ritual purity in eating, drinking, speaking and touching. When finally initiated, the man joins the assembly to bless all who belong to the new covenant and ritually curse all who are not initiates. At this point the leaders reveal the secrets of angelology to the initiates. Josephus states they are to "keep secret the names of the angels."[19]

The account in *The Book of Jubilees* says that God sent the Watchers to earth. It says, "And in the second week of the tenth jubilee Mahalalel took Dinah as a wife. She was the daughter of Barakiel, the daughter of his father's brother, and she bore him a son in the third week of the sixth year. He named him Jared, and in his days the Lord's angels named the Watchers came down to the earth, in order to instruct the humans, and so that they could carry out judgment and justice on the earth." (*Jubilees 4:15*)

Here is the parallel account in *Genesis* 6:1-4: "When humankind began to increase on the face of the earth, and daughters were born to them, those associated with God saw that the human women were beautiful and so they took wives for themselves from any they chose. ...... The Nephilim were on the earth in those times, and also afterwards, when those associated with God were having sex with the human women, who gave birth to their children. They were the mighty heroes of ancient times, the famous ones."

The third century Church Father Commodian said, "When Almighty God, to beautify the nature of the world, willed that that earth should be visited by angels, when they were sent down they despised His laws. Such was the beauty of women, that it turned them aside; so that, being contaminated, they could not return to heaven. Rebels from God, they uttered words against Him. Then the Highest uttered His judgment against them; and from their seed giants are said to have been born. By them arts were made known in the earth, and they taught the dyeing of wool, and everything which is done; and to them, when they died, men erected images. But the Almighty, because they were of an evil seed, did not approve that, when dead, they should be brought back from death. Whence wandering they now subvert many bodies, and it is such as these especially that ye this day worship and pray to as gods." (Translation: A. Cleveland Coxe *et al.*)[20]

The *Septuagint*, Philo of Alexandria, Josephus, Justin Martyr, Irenaeus, Athenagoras, Clement of Alexandria, Tertullian, Lactantius, Eusebius, Ambrose of Milan, Jerome, Sulpicius Severus, and Augustine of Hippo all identified the associates of God of Genesis 6:1-4 with the angels who came to earth and had sex with human women.

Philo, commenting on Genesis 6:2, states, "Those beings which other philosophers call 'demons' are usually called 'angels' by Moses. They are souls hovering in the air. No one should conclude that what is here stated is a fable."[21]

The second century church father, Justin Martyr, stated, "When God had made the entire world, and had put humankind over the matters of the earth, and had arranged the heavenly elements to increase the produce and to rotate the seasons, and had appointed this divine law—for he also did these things for humankind - he committed the care of humans and everything under heaven to angels whom he appointed over them. However, the angels disobeyed this appointment, and were taken by love for women.

"They fathered children who are those that are called demons. Besides that, they later subdued humankind to themselves, partly by magical writings, partly by fear and the punishments they meted out, and partly by teaching them to offer sacrifices, incense, and libations, which is what they needed after they were taken captive by shameless obsessions.

"They caused murders, wars, adulteries, intemperate deeds, and all wickedness among humankind. The poets and the legend-makers, not realising that it was the angels and those demons who had been fathered by the ones that did these things to men and women, cities and nations, which they related, attributed these things to god himself and to those who were ascribed to be his very offspring, and to the offspring of those who were called his brothers, Neptune and Pluto, and also to the children of these their offspring. They called them by whatever name each of the angels had given to himself and his children."[22]

1 Enoch 6 names the leaders of the Watchers: "These are the names of their leaders: Semjaza, who was their leader, Arakiba, Rameel, Kokaqbiel, Ramuel, Tamiel, Ramiel, Danel, Ezeqeel, Baraqijal, Asael, Armaros, Batarerl, Ananel, Zaqiel, Samsapeel, Satarei, Turel, Jomjael, Sariel. These were the leaders of the groups of ten."

The Book of Jubilees 5:6 says, "God was exceedingly angry against the angels he had sent upon the earth."

Here is the account of the *First Book of Enoch 7*.

"They and the rest took consorts. Each one chose their own. They had sex with them and defiled themselves with them. They taught them charms and sorceries, the cutting of roots, and the uses of plants.

"The women got pregnant and gave birth to Nephilim[23] whose height was three hundred cubits. They consumed everything humans produced. When humans could no longer sustain them, they turned against them, in order to consume them. They began to do wrong against birds, beasts, reptiles, and fish, and to eat each other's flesh,[24] and to drink their blood. Then the earth laid accusation against the lawless ones."

In the above passage, the Greek texts of 1 Enoch differ from the Ethiopic. One Greek manuscript adds to this section, "And the women bore to the Watchers three races: first, the great Giants who brought forth the Nephilim, and the Nephilim brought forth the Elioud. And they existed and their power and greatness increased."

Both Romans Chapter 1 and the book of Jude in the New Testament mention "flesh of different kind." The Bible was first translated into English only five hundred years ago, and since then, English Bible translators have guessed that this expression referred to homosexuality. Interesting, they were incorrect, as this expression refers to the Watchers coming to earth and "whoring after" human women. This is well documented in the apocryphal literature. That is, in common literature of the time, it was commonly believed that angels came to earth and had sex with human women.

Let us look at the account of The Watchers in 1 Enoch.

1 Enoch 6:1-8.

"It happened after the humans had multiplied, that in those times daughters were born to them, and they were attractive and beautiful.

"When the angels, the inhabitants of heaven, saw them, they lusted after them and said to each other, 'Come on, let's choose consorts for ourselves from the humans, and let's produce children!'

"Then their leader Semjaza said to them, 'I'm concerned as I fear that perhaps you won't agree to carry out this venture, and that I alone will have to pay the penalty for such a serious crime.'

"But they answered, 'Let's all swear an oath, and bind ourselves by mutual curses, that we will not change our minds but carry through this venture.'

"So they swore all together and bound themselves by mutual curses. They were two hundred in number, they descended in the time of Jared, on the top of Mount Hermon. They called it Mount Hermon because they had sworn an oath on it and bound themselves by mutual curses.[25]

7:1-6.

"They and the rest took consorts. Each one chose their own. They had sex with them and defiled themselves with them. They taught them charms and sorceries, the cutting of roots, and the uses of plants."

"The women got pregnant and gave birth to Nephilim whose height was three hundred cubits. They consumed everything humans produced. When humans could no longer sustain them, they turned against them, in order to consume them. They began to do wrong against birds, beasts, reptiles, and fish, and to eat each other's flesh,[26] and to drink their blood. Then the earth laid accusation against the lawless ones."

8:1-4.

"Azazel taught humans to make swords, knives, shields, breastplates, and showed them metals of the earth and the art of alchemy, and bracelets and ornaments, the use of antimony and paint, the beautifying of the eyelids, the use of all types of precious stones, and all sorts of dyes. Then wickedness and immorality increased, and they disobeyed, and everything they did was corrupt.

Semjaza taught spell potions, and root cuttings,
Armaros taught the resolving of spell potions,
Baraqijal taught astrology,
Kokabel taught the constellations,
Ezeqeel taught the knowledge of the clouds,
Araqiel the signs of the earth,
Shamseil the signs of the sun,
and Sareil the course of the moon.

And as humans perished, they cried out, and their voice reached heaven."

9:1-11.

"Then Michael, Uriel, Raphael, and Gabriel looked down from heaven and saw much bloodshed on earth, and all the lawlessness that was happening on the earth. They said one to another, 'It's the voice of their cries! The earth deprived of her children has cried as far as the portal of heaven. And now people's souls complain to you, you sacred ones of heaven! They say, "Bring our case to the Most High!" Then they said to their Lord, "You are Lord of lords, God of gods, King of kings. Your splendid throne lasts for ever and ever, and is your name is sacred, magnificent, and blessed for ever and ever. You have made everything and you have power over everything, everything is open and clear before you. You see everything, and nothing can be hidden from you.

"You have seen what Azazel has done, how he has taught every lawless act on earth, and has disclosed to the world all the secret things which are done in the heavens which humans were keen to know - also Semjaza, to whom you have given authority over his associates. They have gone together to the human women, have had sex with them, and have defiled themselves, and have revealed these crimes to them. And the women likewise have given birth to Nephilim, and so the whole earth has been filled with blood and lawlessness. And now the souls of those who are dead cry out and complain, even at heaven's portals! Their groaning ascends! It cannot stop due to the lawlessness which is committed on earth.

"You know everything before it happens. You know these things, and what has been done by them, yet you do not tell us what we are supposed to do about it?"

10:1-22.

"Then the Most High, the sacred great one spoke. He sent Uriel to Lamech's son (*Noah*), and said to him, 'Tell him in my name, "Hide yourself!", then explain to him the event that is about to happen, that the whole earth will be destroyed, that a flooding deluge will cover the whole earth, and everything in it will be destroyed. And now tell him how he may escape, and how his descendants may remain for all generations on the earth.

"Again the Lord said to Raphael, 'Bind Azazel hand and foot, cast him into the darkness! Make an opening in the desert which is in Dudael, and throw him in there! Put him on rough and pointed stones, and cover him with darkness. Let him stay there forever, and cover his face so he can't see the light. And in the day of the great judgment he will be thrown into the fire. Restore the earth, which the angels have corrupted, and proclaim life to it, that they may restore it. And all the humans will not perish as a result of all the secrets of the Watchers, and which they have taught to their offspring. All the earth has been corrupted by the works that were taught by Azazel. The blame for the whole crime rests on him!'

"The Lord said to Gabriel, 'Go to the bastards, to the reprobates, to the offspring of immorality, and destroy them, the offspring of the Watchers, from among the humans, and send them against one another so that they will perish by killing one another, for they will not live long lives. No request their fathers make of you will be granted on their behalf. They wish to live eternally but each one of them will live for five hundred years."

"The Lord said to Michael, 'Go and bind Semjaza and his associates who have had sex with women and so have completely polluted and contaminated themselves! And when their sons have slain one another, and they have seen the destruction of their beloved ones, bind them for seventy generations under the earth, until the day of their judgment and of their end, until the judgment that lasts forever is completed. In those times they will be taken away to the lowest depths of the fire and tormented and they will be shut up in prison forever. Immediately after this he will, together with them, be condemned and destroyed, and they will be bound together for generation after generations.

"Destroy all the lustful spirits, and the offspring of the Watchers, for they have committed crimes against humankind. Let all oppressors perish from the face of the earth and let every evil work be destroyed. Let the plant of justice and truth appear and become a blessing. Justice and truth will be forever planted with enjoyment.

"And then all the devoted people will be thankful, and live until they have produced a thousand children, while the whole time of their youth, and their old age, will come to an end peacefully.

"In those times the whole earth will be cultivated with justice, and will be planted with trees and be filled with blessings. And all desirable trees will be planted on it. They will plant vines on it. The vines which they plant will yield abundant wine. Every seed which is sown on it will produce a thousand measures for one measure, and produce ten presses of oil for one measure of olives.

"Cleanse the earth from all oppression, from all injustice, from all crimes, from all godlessness, and from all the pollution which is committed on it. Eliminate them from the earth. Then all the humans will be just, and all nations will highly respect me and bless me, and all will esteem me. The earth will be cleansed from all defilement, from every crime, from all punishment, and from all torment, and I will never again send torment on it for generation after generation, forever."

The Book of Jude in the New Testament mentions the three elements that are linked in accounts of the Watchers, sorcery, going after a different flesh, and punishment of angels. Jude quotes *1 Enoch* in verses 14-15:

"And as for the Messengers who did not uphold their own office but deserted their own places, he has held them firmly in eternal ropes down in the gloom, waiting for the Judgment of the Great Day. Just like these, Sodom and Gomorrah as well as the surrounding cities, which in a similar way committed *porneia* and went after different flesh,[27] serve as an example of those who undergo punishment in the eternal fire."

The Book of Jubilees 7:20-22 states, "Noah… encouraged his sons…to avoid *porneia*, uncleanness, and injustice. For it was on account of these three things that the flood came on the earth, since it was due to *porneia* in which the Watchers, against the regulations of their authority, had illicit sex and went a whoring after human women. When they married whomever they liked, they committed the first acts of uncleanness. They fathered as children the Nephilim."

The *Book of Jubilees* 4:22 says, "And he testified about the Watchers, who had sinned with the female humans, for they had begun to sleep with the female humans causing defilement, and Enoch testified against them all."

The *Book of Jubilees* 5:1-4 states that when humans increased, that God's angels chose any human females they wanted, and that the progeny were called Nephilim.

The *Testament of Naphtali* 3.3.4-5 states that the women of Sodom had sex with the Watchers. It states, "In the same way also the Watchers changed the order of their nature. The Lord cursed the Watchers at the flood, and made the earth desolate because of them, so that it would be uninhabited and fruitless." Note the term "changed the order of their nature" which is similar to Jude's term, "went after different flesh" and to Paul's statement, "for the females exchanged natural sex for what is other than nature. And the same goes for males too," in Romans 1:26.

The Church Father Irenaeus stated, "And wickedness very long-continued and widespread pervaded all the races of men, until very little seed of justice was in them. For unlawful unions came about on earth, as angels linked themselves with offspring of the daughters of men, who bore to them sons, who on account of their exceeding great were called Giants. The angels, then, brought to their wives as gifts teachings of evil, for they taught them the virtues of roots and herbs, and dyeing and cosmetics and discoveries of precious materials, love-philtes, hatreds, amours, passions, constraints of love, the bonds of witchcraft, every sorcery and idolatry, hateful to God, and when this was come into the world, the affairs of wickedness were propagated to overflowing, and those of justice dwindled to very little."[28]

The *Genesis Apocryphon* (*1QapGen*), one of the Dead Sea Scrolls texts, mentions the angels breeding with human women. Lamech questions his tearful wife as he suspects that Noah's biological father may have been an angel or a Nephilim.[29]

The second century theologian Tatian, 2 *Apology* 5, stated, "God committed the care of humans and everything under heaven to angels whom he appointed over them. But the angels disobeyed this appointment, and were captivated by the love of women. They produced children who are called demons, and not only that, they later subjugated the human race for themselves, partly by magical writings, partly by fears and the punishments they brought about, and partly by teaching them to offer sacrifices, incense, and libations, as they needed these things after they were enslaved by lust. Among humankind they sowed murders, wars, adulteries, awful actions, and all kinds of wickedness."

Clement of Alexandria, *Miscellanies* 5.1.10 stated, "To this we will also add, that the angels who had obtained the superior rank, after sinking into pleasures, told the women the secrets which had come to their knowledge."

2 Enoch 10 states, "Those two men led me up on to the north side, and showed me there an awful place. There were all kinds of tortures in that place, brutal darkness and the gloom of darkness. There is no light there, but a gloomy fire constantly burning high, and a fiery river coming out. The whole place is on fire, and everywhere there is frost, ice, thirst, and cold. The bonds are very cruel, and the angels frightening and without compassion. They carry fierce weapons and harsh torture. I said, "Woe, woe, this place is so awful!" And those men replied, "Enoch, this place is prepared for those who dishonor God, who on earth practice crime against nature, child-corruption, magic-making, enchantments, and devilish witchcrafts, and who boast of their wicked deeds, stealing, lies, slander, envy, resentment, *porneia*, murder. They are accursed and steal people's lives, and take away the possessions of the poor in order to make themselves rich, harming them, and although they are able to feed the hungry, make them starve to death, and although they can clothe people, they strip them naked. They did not acknowledge their creator, and bowed down to the soulless and lifeless gods who cannot see nor hear, useless gods, and they also built carved images and bowed down to unclean work. This whole place is prepared for their eternal inheritance."

2 Enoch speaks of those who "practice crime against nature." In similar language in Romans 1, Paul speaks of those who "exchanged God's truth for the lie, the idol, and worshipped and served the creation other than the Creator… the females exchanged natural sex for what is other than nature. And the same goes for males too. The males got rid of natural sex with the female and burned with their mutual yearning – males producing indecency with one another, and as a result got what was coming to them for their mistake. They didn't think it fit to acknowledge God, so he gave them an unfit mind, to do things that are not appropriate. They have been filled with every kind of wrongdoing, evil, greedy grasping behavior, malice - full to the utmost with jealousy, murder, quarrels, deceit, nasty dispositions. They are people who give out information, whether true or false, which is detrimental to the character or welfare of others. They are slanderers, God haters, insolent, arrogant, boastful, inventors of bad deeds. They are not obedient to parents, they don't have intelligence, they do not keep covenant, they do not have natural affection, they do not have mercy."

Jude speaks of angels who did not uphold their own office, and that God has held them with eternal ropes down in the gloom. In the next sentence Jude says that "just like these" Sodom and Gomorrah "who went after different flesh" serve as an example of those who undergo punishment in the eternal fire.

The "different flesh" of Jude is usually taken by Christians to be about homosexuality, but in fact it was about sex between angels and humans.

Jude quotes 1 Enoch in verses 14-15. 1 Enoch 6-10 states that 200 angels came to earth, lusted after human women causing "defilement" and producing progeny. *The Book of Jubilees* 5 sets out God's punishment on these angels. 2 Enoch 10 states, "And (they)… showed me there a very terrible place, and there were all manner of tortures in that place: cruel darkness and unillumined gloom, and there is no light there, but murky fire constantly flaming aloft, and there is a fiery river coming forth, and that whole place is everywhere fire, and everywhere there is frost and ice, thirst and shivering, while the bonds are very cruel... This place is reserved for those who sin against nature." Note the words "sin against nature" which we also see in Romans 1.

The context in Romans 1 and Jude is angels having sex with humans, as well as committing other crimes. In fact, the context cannot be more obvious in Jude 6-7, "And as for the Messengers (angels) who did not uphold their own office but deserted their own places, he (the Lord) has held them firmly in eternal ropes down in the gloom, waiting for the Judgment of the Great Day. Just like these, Sodom and Gomorrah as well as the surrounding cities, which in a similar way committed *porneia* and went after different flesh, serve as an example of those who undergo punishment in the eternal fire." 1 Enoch 10 says the main angel who was responsible for abandoning his office in this way was bound hand and foot and cast into in darkness where he would remain until the Great Day of Judgment.

Note the "just like these" in verse 7. Jude is spelling it out very clearly: certain angels did not uphold their own office, are held with ropes in darkness/gloom, and just like these, Sodom and Gomorrah went after strange flesh (that is, angels having sex with human women). This is most certainly nothing to do with homosexuality: it is not even anything at all to do with sex between human beings.

The Bible clearly states that the flood was due to the behavior of the Watchers. They are referred to in Genesis as "those associated with Elohim," Elohim being one of the Hebrew words translated as "God" by many Bible versions.

Genesis 6.

1 When humankind began to multiply on the face of the earth, and daughters were born to them,

2 those associated with Elohim saw that the human women were beautiful, and so they took wives for themselves from any they chose.

3 So Yahweh said, "My spirit will not remain with humankind indefinitely, since they are mortal. They will remain for 120 more years."

4 The Nephilim were on the earth in those times, and also afterwards, when those associated with Elohim were having sex with the human women, who gave birth to their children. They were the mighty heroes of ancient times, the famous ones.

5 But Yahweh saw that the wickedness of humankind was abundant on the earth. Every thought and purpose in their minds was nothing but evil all the time.

6 Yahweh regretted that he had made humankind on the earth, and he was very upset.

7 So Yahweh said, "I will wipe out humankind, whom I have created, off the face of the earth – everything from humankind to animals, including reptiles and birds, as I am sorry I have made them."

8 But Noah found favor in Yahweh's sight.

9 This is the account of Noah.
Noah was a just man and he was blameless
among his contemporaries. He walked with Elohim.

10 Noah had three sons: Shem, Ham, and Japheth.

11 The earth was ruined in Elohim's sight; the earth was filled with violence.

12 Elohim saw the earth, and indeed it was ruined, for all living creatures on the earth were sinful.

13 So Elohim said to Noah, "I have decided that all living creatures must die, for the earth is filled with violence because of them. Now I am about to destroy them and the earth.

14 Make an ark of cypress wood for yourself."

The *Book of Jubilees* 5 sets out the punishment by God upon the Watchers and specifically says that the flood was due to the

Watchers taking human wives but that God saved Noah from it. It says that the flood came on the earth due to *porneia*, uncleanness, and injustice, and that it was due to *porneia* in which the Watchers had illicit sex with human women.

Many Christians today think Sodom was destroyed because of homosexuality. Let us have a look now at every mention (apart from where the name is just mentioned in passing) of Sodom in the Bible to see precisely what the Bible says about this matter.

Before we do that, I will remind you that Sodom is mentioned in 1 Enoch:14-15 which states,

"And as for the Messengers who did not uphold their own office but deserted their own places, he has held them firmly in eternal ropes down in the gloom, waiting for the Judgment of the Great Day. Just like these, Sodom and Gomorrah as well as the surrounding cities, which in a similar way committed *porneia* and went after different flesh, serve as an example of those who undergo punishment in the eternal fire."

The "going after different flesh" refers of course to the angels ("the Watchers", "those associated with God") having sex with human women.

Porneia is a term referring to acts condemned in the Law of Moses, acts encompassing idolatry and/or pornography, vice, certain sexual acts. There is no equivalent English term. Leviticus 18 lists idolatry and ritually unclean sexual acts against the laws of Moses, and in 18:3 states, "You must not do the deeds of the land of Canaan into which I am about to bring you." These included incest, sex with in-laws, sex with a woman as a rival to her sister, women or men having sex with animals, child offerings to Molech, sex with a woman during menstruation. Note also that the polytheistic Canaanites were particularly despised in the Old Testament, and male temple prostitution was part of their worship of their goddess Asherah. Cult prostitution and eunuchs castrating themselves (and thereafter dressing in women's clothing, as in Deuteronomy 22:5) both figured in the worship of the Canaanite goddess Astarte.

Here *porneia* refers to the Watchers' union with human woman, a ritual abomination.

Let us turn to the Hebrew Bible/Old Testament.

Genesis 18:20.
And Yahweh said, "Because the cry of Sodom and Gomorrah is great, and because their sin is very serious, I will go down now and see whether they have done that which the outcry against it that has come to me says it has done, and if not, I will know."

Isaiah 13:19-22.
19 Babylon, the most admired of kingdoms,
the Chaldeans' source of honor and pride, will be destroyed by God just as Sodom and Gomorrah were.
20 No one will live there again;
no one will ever reside there again.
No Arabian will camp there,
no shepherds will rest their flocks there.
21 But the desert dwellers will recline there, and their dwellings will be full of howling creatures, and female unclean birds will live there, and hairy goat demons (*se'irim*) will dance there.
22 The howlers will answer in their desolate dwellings,
and dragons in their delightful temples.
Her time is almost up,
and her days will not be prolonged.

Interestingly, verse 21 mentions hairy goat demons (*se'irim*). The 13th century Nahmanides' (Rabbi Moses ben Nachman's) commentary on Leviticus 26:8 states that Azazel belongs to the class of *se'irim*, hairy goat like demons. This follows Rabbi Abraham ibn Ezra's commentary although Ibn Ezra did not state this explicitly. Isaiah 34:15 states, "The wild animals of the desert will meet with the howlers, and the hairy goat demon (*se'irim*) will cry to its fellow. Lilith will settle there and find for herself a resting place."

Jeremiah 23:13-14.
13 The Lord says, "I saw the prophets of Samaria doing something that was foolish. They prophesied in the name of Baal and mislead my people Israel.
14 I have seen the prophets of Jerusalem doing something horrible. They are unfaithful to me and continually prophesy lies.

"They strengthen the power of evildoers, with the result that they do not stop their wickedness. They are all like Sodom to me and its inhabitants like Gomorrah."

Jeremiah **49:18.**

"Edom will be destroyed like Sodom and Gomorrah and the neighboring towns, says the Lord. "No one will live there. No human being will settle in it."

Jeremiah **50:40.**

"I will destroy Babylonia just like I did Sodom and Gomorrah and the neighboring towns," says the Lord, "no one will live there. No human being will settle in it."

Lamentations **4:6.**

The punishment of my people exceeded the penalty of Sodom, which was overthrown in a moment with no one to help her.

Ezekiel **16:14-58.**

20 You took your sons and your daughters whom you bore to me and you killed them as sacrifice to be eaten. Were your acts of harlotry not enough?

21 You sacrificed my children and gave them up as sacrificial offerings.

22 In all your abominations and your whorings you did not remember the days of your youth when you were naked and bare, and were desecrated by bloodguilt.

23 After all your evil ("Woe! Woe to you!" says Adonai Yahweh)

24 you built yourself a brothel and put up a place consecrated to the worship of idols in every public square.

25 You put up a place consecrated to the worship of idols at the top of every road and you made your beauty a ritual abomination when you spread your legs to every passer by and multiplied your acts of harlotry.

26 You played the harlot with the Egyptians, your sexually aroused neighbors, multiplying your acts of harlotry and making me angry.

27 So then, I have stretched out my hand against you and cut off your rations. I have delivered you over to the will of those who hate you, the daughters of the Philistines, who were ashamed by your obscene behavior.

28 You played the harlot with the Assyrians because your sexual desires were insatiable; you played the harlot with them and yet you were still not satisfied.

29 Then you multiplied your acts of harlotry with the merchant land of Chaldea, but even then you were not satisfied.

30 How feeble is your heart, says Adonai Yahweh, to do such things, the acts of a bold harlot!

31 When you built yourself a brothel and put up a place consecrated to the worship of idols in every public square, you were not seen as a harlot, because you scoffed at payment.

32 But you are like an adulterous wife, who prefers strangers to her own husband.

33 They give payment to all harlots, but instead you give gifts to all your lovers and bribed them to come to you from all around for your sexual favors!

34 You were different from other harlots because no one solicited you. You are the opposite, because you gave payment and no payment was given to you.

35 So, harlot, hear Yahweh's word!

36 This is what Adonai Yahweh says: Because your lust was poured out and you exposed your nakedness in your harlotry with your lovers, and because of all your detestable idols, and because you have given them your children's blood,

37 so then, take note: I will gather all your lovers you slept with, both all those you loved and all those you hated. I will gather them against you from all around, and I will expose your nakedness to them, and they will see all your nakedness.

38 I will punish you as one who commits adultery and idolatrous worship, and as one who sheds blood deserves. I will avenge your bloody deeds with furious rage.

39 I will hand you over to them and they will destroy your brothels and tear down your places consecrated to the worship of idols. They will strip you of your clothing and take your beautiful jewelry and leave you naked and bare.

40 They will bring a mob that will stone you and cut you to pieces with their swords.

41 They will burn down your houses and execute judgments on you in front of many women. I will make you stop paying the whore, and you will no longer give gifts to your lovers.

42 My anger to you will subside, and my jealousy will turn from you. I will calm down and no longer be angry.

43 Because you did not remember the times of your youth and have enraged me with all these deeds, I will surely repay you for what you have done, says Adonai Yahweh. Have you not played the harlot on top of all your other abominations?

44 Certainly, everyone who quotes proverbs will quote this proverb about you: "Like mother, like daughter."

45 You are the daughter of your mother, who hated her husband and her children, and you are the sister of your sisters who hated their husbands and their children. Your mother was a Hittite and your father an Amorite.

46 Your older sister was Samaria, who lived north of you with her daughters, and your younger sister, who lived south of you with her daughters, was Sodom.

47 Have you not copied their behavior and practiced their ritual abominations? In a short time you became even more ruined then they in all your ways!

48 As surely as I live, says Adonai Yahweh, your sister Sodom and her daughters never did what you and your daughters have done.

49 See here – this was the guilt of your sister Sodom: she and her daughters had excellence, plenty of food, and were peacefully prosperous, but they did not help the poor and needy.

50 They exalted themselves and practiced ritual abominations in front of me. So then when I saw that I removed them.

51 Samaria did not commit half the sins you did; you have done more ritual abominations than they did. You have made your sisters appear just with all the ritual abominations you have done.

52 So now, bear your disgrace, because you have given your sisters reason to justify their behavior. Because the sins you have committed were more abominable than those of your sisters; they have become more just than you. So now, be ashamed and bear the disgrace of making your sisters appear just.

53 I will restore their fortunes, the fortunes of Sodom and her daughters, and the fortunes of Samaria and her daughters, and I will restore your fortunes among them,

54 so that you may bear your disgrace and be ashamed of everything you have done in comforting them.

55 As for your sisters, Sodom and her daughters will be restored to their former status, Samaria and her daughters will be restored to their former status, and you and your daughters will be restored to your former status.

56 In your days of majesty, you would not even mention Sodom,

57 before your wickedness was exposed. Now you have become an object of scorn to the daughters of Aram and all those around her, and to the daughters of the Philistines – those all around you who despise you.

58 You must bear your punishment for your idolatry and harlotry and your ritual abominations, says Yahweh.

Amos 4:11.

"I overthrew some of you the way Elohim overthrew Sodom and Gomorrah. You were like a brand plucked out of the flames, yet you did not return to me," says Yahweh.

Zephaniah 2:9.

"Therefore, as surely as I live," says Yahweh who commands armies, Elohim of Israel, "Moab shall become like Sodom, and the Ammonites like Gomorrah, a land overrun by reeds and salt pits, and a wasteland forever. Those of my people who are left will plunder their belongings, and those who are left in Judah will possess their land."

Here are the New Testament mentions of Sodom.

Matthew 10:15.

Let me make this clear, the land of Sodom and Gomorrah will be better off in the Day of Judgment than that city!

Matthew **11:20-24.**

20 "Then Jesus began to reproach the cities in which he had done powerful things, because they didn't change their minds. *21* "Woe to you, Korazin, woe to you Bethsaida! If the powerful things done in you had been done in Tyre and Sidon, they would have changed their minds long ago! They would have dressed in rags and put ashes on their heads to show they were sorry! *22* Tyre and Sidon will be better off than you in the Day of Judgment! *23* And you, Capernaum, will you be lifted up to heaven? No! You will be brought down to Hades, because if the powerful things done in you had been done in Sodom, Sodom would still be here today! *24* The land of Sodom will be better off than you in the Day of Judgment!

Luke **10:12.**

8 "When you go into a city and they welcome you, eat what they put in front of you. *9* Heal the sick there and tell them, 'God's Realm is close to you.' *10* But when you go to a city and they don't welcome you, go into the streets and say, *11* 'The very dust of your city which sticks to our feet we wipe off against you! Only realize this - God's Realm is nearby!' *12* I tell you - Sodom will be better off on that day than that city!

Luke **17:29.**

26 "The Human Being's time will be the same as it was in Noah's time. *27* People were eating, drinking, marrying, up to the very time that Noah went into the ark. Then the flood came and wiped them all out. *28* It was the same in the time of Lot. People were eating and drinking, buying and selling, planting and building. *29* But the very day that Lot left Sodom, fire and sulfur rained down on them from the sky and wiped them all out."

Romans **9:29.**

And just as Isaiah has foretold, "Unless the Lord of Armies had left us a seed, we would have become like Sodom, and we would have made like Gomorrah."

2 Peter **2:4-6.**

4 God didn't spare the Messengers (= angels) who sinned but handed them over to Tartarus in ropes in the underworld's gloom where they are firmly held for judgment. *5* God did not spare the ancient world, but guarded Noah, a preacher of justice, and seven others, when he brought the flood upon those who committed sacrilege. *6* God condemned the cities of Sodom and Gomorrah, reducing them to ashes and a sudden end, as an example of what's in store for those who commit sacrilege.

Revelation 11:7-8.

7 When they have finished their testimony, the beast that comes up from the abyss will attack them, conquer them and kill them. *8* Their corpses will lie in the street of the great city, which is spiritually called Sodom and Egypt, where their Lord was also crucified.

Let us now focus on the statements as to why Sodom was destroyed. There are three such statements in the Bible, in Ezekiel 16:49-50, in 2 Peter 2:6, and in Jude 1:7. I have quoted Ezekiel 16:14-58 above so you can see the whole context. Now let us turn to Ezekiel 16:49-50.

Ezekiel 16:49-50.

49 See here – this was the guilt of your sister Sodom: she and her daughters had excellence, plenty of food, and were peacefully prosperous, but they did not help the poor and needy.
50 They exalted themselves and practiced ritual abominations in front of me. So then when I saw that I removed them.

There is a comment that Sodom had excellence (sometimes mistranslated as "pride"), plenty of food, and were peacefully prosperous, but they did not help the poor and needy. However, this was not given as the reason that Sodom was destroyed; this was simply the back-story, some extra information about Sodom. The reason is given in verse 50. "They exalted themselves and practiced ritual abominations in front of me. So then when I saw that I removed them."

2 Peter **2:6.**

4 God didn't spare the Messengers who sinned but handed them over to Tartarus in ropes in the underworld's gloom where they are firmly held for judgment. *5* God did not spare the ancient world, but guarded Noah, a preacher of justice, and seven others, when he brought the flood upon those who committed sacrilege. *6* God condemned the cities of Sodom and Gomorrah, reducing them to ashes and a sudden end, as an example of what's in store for those who commit sacrilege.

Jude **1:6-7.**

6 And as for the Messengers who did not uphold their own office but deserted their own places, he has held them firmly in eternal ropes down in the gloom, waiting for the Judgment of the Great Day. *7* Just like these, Sodom and Gomorrah as well as the surrounding cities, which in a similar way committed *porneia* and went after different flesh, serve as an example of those who undergo punishment in the eternal fire.

Both Peter and Jude said that Sodom was destroyed as an example for those who commit sacrilege/*porneia*, which they stated to be the angels (Watchers) going after "different flesh."

This spells it out clearly – Sodom was destroyed for the practice of ritual abominations (translated by the *Septuagint* as "lawbreaking").

What were these ritual abominations? The *Testament of Naphtali* 3.3.4-5 states that the women of Sodom had sex with the Watchers. It states, "In the same way also the Watchers changed the order of their nature. The Lord cursed the Watchers at the flood, and made the earth desolate because of them, so that it would be uninhabited and fruitless." Note again the term "changed the order of their nature" which is similar to Jude's term, "went after different flesh" and to Paul's statement, "for the females exchanged natural sex for what is other than nature. And the same goes for males too," in Romans 1:26.

Chapter 4. Punishment of the Watchers.

The Book of Jubilees 4:22 5:1-4 states that Enoch testified against the Watchers, who had sinned with the female humans. It states that the human women bore children called "Nephilim" to the Watchers.

The Book of Jubilees 5 tells us that God was furiously angry with the angels he had sent to the earth. It sets out the punishment by God upon the Watchers and says that the flood was due to the Watchers taking human wives but that God saved Noah from it.

"When the humans began to increase on the earth and daughters were born to them, on a certain year of this jubilee, the angels of God saw that they were beautiful to look at and they took for themselves any woman they chose. The women bore progeny to them and they were Nephilim.[30] Lawlessness increased on the earth and all living things went corrupt, humans, cattle, animals, birds, and everything that walks on the earth - they went corrupt in every way and started eating each other. Lawlessness increased on the earth. People's thoughts were always evil, and this kept happening

"God looked at the earth, and it was corrupt. Every living thing had gone corrupt. Everything on the earth had done all kinds of evil as far as God was concerned. God said that he would destroy humans and all living things on the face of the earth which he had created. But Noah found favor in the Lord's eyes.

"God was furious with the angels he had sent to the earth. He was exceedingly angry. He gave the order to strip them completely of their authority. He told us to bind them in the depths of the earth. So they are bound there in the middle of the earth, and are kept separate.

"God also commanded that their offspring were to be put to the sword, and be removed from under heaven. God said, "My spirit will not always stay with humans, as they are also flesh and blood, and they will live to the age of one hundred and twenty years."

"God sent his sword amongst them so that each would slay their neighbor. They kept killing each other until they all fell by the sword and were wiped off the face of the earth. Their fathers[31] were witnesses to this. After this happened their fathers were bound in the depths of the earth until the day of the great condemnation, when judgment will be executed on all those who have done corrupt things in the Lord's sight. The Lord expelled them from their lands.

"Not one of them judged by the Lord as wicked was left. The Lord made a new honorable nature for his whole creation, so that their nature would not be wholly evil, but everyone would always act in an honorable way. The judgment of everyone is justly ordained and written on the heavenly tablets, that is to say, the judgment of all who do not behave the way in which it is ordained for them to behave. Judgment is written down for every creature and for every kind that does not behave honorably. There is nothing in heaven or on earth, or in light or in darkness, or in Sheol or in the depth, or in the place of darkness which is not judged. All their judgments are ordained, written, and engraved. He will judge everything, the important, the insignificant, each after their own way."

The punishment of the Watchers is also featured in 2 Peter 2:4-8. The passage there is about the Watchers who came down to earth and rebelled against God's ordinances by whoring after human women (including those of Sodom and Gomorrah, cf. *Testament of Naphtali* 3.3.4-5).

"God didn't spare the Messengers who sinned but handed them over to Tartarus in ropes in the underworld's gloom where they are firmly held for judgment."

As mentioned earlier, *1 Enoch* 10:1-22 tells us about the punishment of the Watchers. Raphael was told to bind Azazel's hands and feet, and to throw him into the darkness in an opening in the desert in Dudael. He was to be thrown onto rough, pointed stones and have his face covered so he could not see the light. Azazel was condemned to stay there forever. Worse still, he was to be thrown into the fire on the day of judgment.

Matthew 25:41 says, "Then he will say to those on the left side, 'Get out of my sight, you doubly cursed ones! Off you go, into the permanent fire prepared for *the diabolos* (the slanderer-liar) and his messengers!'"

Gabriel was ordered to wipe out the offspring of the Watchers, and to set them against one another so that they would kill one another.

Michael was ordered to bind Semjaza and his associates who had sex with the human women. After Semjaza and his associates witnessed the death of their offspring, they were to be bound together under the earth for seventy generations. They were to be tormented and they will be shut up in prison forever.

In the New Testament, the passage in *2 Peter* 2:4-8 is about the Watchers: "God didn't spare the angels who sinned but handed them over to Tartarus in ropes in the underworld's gloom where they are firmly held for judgment."

The ancient accounts agree that the Fallen Angels were thrown into Tartarus to be punished. The words "Gehenna", "Hades" and "Tartarus", three very different places in the Greek, are usually all just (mis)translated as "Hell" in most Bible versions. Gehenna was a real place on earth. It was the Jerusalem rubbish dump, and was just outside the city. Smoke went up from it at all times as the rubbish was burning continually. It was full of maggots, and the bodies of the worst criminals were thrown there. Josiah used it for the burning of offal. It used to be the site of sacrifice to Molech.

The Greeks considered Hades to be the underworld, full of ghosts or wraiths of people who had died. Homer's *Odyssey* speaks of Odysseus raising spirits from Hades and notes that these spirits could be strengthened when they drank blood. It also speaks of people continuing their earthly ways – for example, one person was hunting. It was spoken of as a terrifying, eerie place, but not a place of punishment like Tartarus. Hades is commonly translated as "Hell" in most Bible versions, as are "Gehenna" and "Tartarus", yet to the Greeks, they were separate places. Tartarus was the lowest region of the underworld, said to be as far below Hades as the earth is under the sky. Tartarus was the place where the very wicked were punished. Hades was simply the afterplace of the dead,[32] whereas Tartarus was a place of severe punishment.

Tartarus was the depths of the underworld, far below Hades. In fact, the Greeks believed Hades was midway between heaven and Tartarus. See classical Greek playwright, Aeschylus, *Prometheus Vinctus*, 152-6: "Would that he had hurled me underneath the earth and underneath the House of Hades, host to the dead – yes, down to limitless Tartarus, yes, though he bound me cruelly in chains breakable." (Trans. David Grene.)

Here is a mention of Tartarus in Homer.

Homer, *Iliad* 8.1.

Now when saffron-robed Dawn was spreading over the face of the who earth, Zeus who hurls the thunderbolt gathered the gods on the highest peak of many-ridged Olympus. He himself addressed their gathering; and all the gods listened to what he had to say. "Listen to me, all you gods and goddesses; I am going to say what my heart in chest bids me to say. No goddess, or god for that matter, is to try to impede my plan, but you all alike are to agree to this, so that I can bring these deeds to pass with great haste. If I see any of you gods breaking rank and going to help either the Trojans or Danaans, you will be assailed in no uncertain manner and sent back to Olympus, or I will get you and throw you into gloomy Tartarus, far, far away, where is the deepest pit below the earth, the gates of which are of iron and the threshold bronze, as far below Hades as heaven is above the earth."

The *Septuagint* translated Sheol as "Hades." The Christian view of a hell ruled by "Satan" and demons has no foundation whatsoever in the Bible. It does say wicked spirits will end up in Tartarus, but as victims not rulers. However, the Christian view of hell does correspond with the fictitious work of John Milton's *Paradise Lost* written in 1667. The beginning of *Paradise Lost* features the fallen angels along with their leader Satan waking up in Hell after having been defeated in the war in heaven. Milton depicts Hell as the residence of the demons.

In *Paradise Lost*, Satan organizes his followers and is helped by his lieutenants named Mammon and Beelzebub.

The place of the afterlife for both the good and the bad in the Hebrew Bible / Old Testament was Sheol. Enoch also speaks of Sheol as a place where the unjust and just end up in the afterlife. Enoch says that in Sheol, good, happiness, and honor are prepared for the just but there is torment for the most wicked.

Basically, the Hebrew Bible / Old Testament speaks of Sheol simply as a place of afterlife. Psalm 139:8 says, "If I were to ascend to heaven, you would be there. If I were to lie in Sheol, you would be there." Sheol is also used as a term to express the end of life, that is, death.

Jewish thought does not see Sheol as a place of punishment inhabited by a leader of demons. This view is specifically that of later times Christianity.

The *First Book of Enoch* 20:1-8 states that Uriel, one of the sacred angels, an archangel, is in charge of Tartarus. Uriel is always depicted as a good angel and not a fallen Angel.

In the next chapter, 1 Enoch elaborates on the punishment of the Watchers. "Then I went to a place where things were dreadful. There I saw neither a high heaven nor an established earth, but a desolate appalling spot. There I saw seven stars of heaven bound together in it, like great mountains of blazing fire. I said, "For what type of crime have they been bound, and why have they been thrown into this place?"

"Then Uriel, one of the sacred angels who was with me, and who guided me, answered, "Enoch, why do you ask, why do you earnestly inquire? These are those of the stars which have disobeyed the Lord's commandment, and are bound here until ten thousand years, the time of their crimes, have come to pass."

"Afterwards I went on from there to another dreadful place, more ghastly than the former, where I saw a huge blazing and glittering fire, in the middle of which there was a split as far as the abyss. It was full of huge columns of fire, and their descent was deep. I could not discover its measurement or magnitude, nor could I perceive its source. Then I exclaimed, "How horrifying this place is, and how difficult to explore!"

Then Uriel, one of the sacred angels who was with me, answered me, "Enoch, why are you alarmed and amazed at this appalling place, at the sight of this place of pain?" He told me, "This is the prison of the angels, and they are kept here for ever."

Chapter 5. Individual Fallen Angels

Here is the account of the Leader of the Watchers in 2 Enoch. Bear in mind "Grigori" is the ancient Greek word for "Watchers."

"These are the Grigori, who with their chief Satanail rejected the Lord of light, and after them are those who are held in the great darkness on the second heaven, and three of them went down on earth to the place Hermon, and broke their vows on the shoulder of the Mount Hermon and saw the human women, and slept with them, and contaminated the earth with their deeds. In their times they caused lawless mixing, and Nephilim were born, amazing big people, and great hostility. So God judged them strongly, and they weep for their associates. They will be punished on the Lord's great day." (*2 Enoch 18:3-4.*)

Here is the account in **Psalm 82**.
A psalm of Asaph.
1 Elohim presides over the assembly of El,[33]
he gives judgment in the midst of the elohim:[34]
2 "How long will you defend the unjust
and show favoritism to the wicked? *Selah*
3 Defend the cause of the poor and the fatherless,
defend the rights of the oppressed and suffering.
4 Rescue the poor and needy,
rescue them from the power of the wicked.
5 They know nothing, they understand nothing,
they walk around in the dark,
all the foundations of the earth are shaken.
6 I said, 'You are elohim,
all of you are associates of Elyon.'
7 Yet you will die like mortals,
you will fall like the other rulers."
8 Rise up, Elohim, and judge the earth,
for you own all the nations.

Here is the account in *Isaiah* 14:12-21.

"How you are fallen from heaven, Lucifer,[35] associate of dawn! How you are cut down to the ground, you who weakened the nations!"

"For you said to yourself, 'I will ascend to heaven and set my throne above El's stars. I will preside on the appointed mountain in the sides of the north. I will climb to above the height of the clouds, I will be like Elyon.'

"But instead, you will be brought down to Sheol, to the sides of the pit. Everyone there will stare at you and ask, 'Is this the one who shook the earth and the kingdoms of the world, that made the world a wilderness and demolished its cities and did not free the prisoners from Sheol?'

"The kings of the nations lie in splendid tombs, but you will be thrown out of your grave like a ritually abominable branch. You will be dumped like the remainder of those slain by the sword with those killed in battle like a corpse trampled underfoot, you will go down to the dungeon. You will not be given a proper burial, because you have destroyed your land and killed your people. The offspring of evildoers will never be proclaimed. Kill the children of this wrongdoer so they do not rise and conquer the land or rebuild the cities of the world."

Here is the account in *Ezekiel* 28:11-19.

"The word of Yahweh came to me, 'Human, weep for the king of Tyre and say to him, "Adonai Yahweh says, 'You were full of wisdom and beauty. You were in Eden, Elohim's garden. Your clothing had every precious stone: sardius, chrysolite, diamond, beryl, onyx, jasper, sapphire, and emerald, carbuncle, gold, and the making of the settings was crafted for you on the day you were created.

'You are the anointed cherub that defends. You had access to Elohim's sacred mountain and walked among the fiery stones. You were complete in everything you did from the day you were created until the day injustice was found in you.

'Your great wealth filled you with violence, and you sinned. So I banished you from Elohim's mountain. Mighty guardian, I expelled you from your place among the fiery stones. Your heart was filled with pride because of your beauty. You corrupted your wisdom because of your splendor. So I threw you to the earth and exposed you to the gaze of kings.

'You defiled your sanctuaries with your many wrongdoings and your dishonest trade. So I brought fire from within you, and it consumed you. I will burn you to ashes on the ground in the sight of all who are watching. All who knew you are appalled at your destruction. You have come to a terrible end, and you are no more."

Here is the account in *Luke* 10:17-20.

The seventy came back and were very happy. They said, "Lord, even the demons yield to us in your name!"

"Yes, I know," Jesus replied. "I was watching Adversary fall like a flash of lightning from the sky. I have given you the authority to trample on snakes and scorpions, and authority over all the enemy's power, and nothing will harm you. But all that aside, don't be happy just because the spirits yield to you, but instead be happy that your names have been written down in the heavenly places."

Here is the account in *Revelation*.

Ch.12:1-2 And a mighty sign appeared in heaven. It was a woman clothed with the sun, with the moon under her feet and a crown of twelve stars on her head. *2* She was pregnant, and cried out in torture as she was in labor and about to give birth.

3-6 And I saw another sign in heaven. It was a huge red dragon with seven heads, ten horns, and seven diadems on the heads! *4* Its tail dragged a third of the stars out of the sky and hurled them to the earth. The dragon stood in front of the woman who was about to give birth, so that he could eat her child the moment it was born. *5* She gave birth to a son, who is destined to rule all the nations with an iron rod. Her child was snatched away and carried up to God and to his throne. *6* The woman escaped into the desert to a place that God had prepared for her, so that she would be taken care of for 1,260 days.

7-9 War broke out in heaven. Michael and his Messengers waged war against the dragon, and the dragon and his messengers fought back. *8* But the dragon wasn't strong enough, and thus they no longer had a place in heaven. *9* The mighty dragon was thrown down - that ancient snake called "Slanderer-Liar", and also called

"Adversary", who leads the whole earth astray. He and his Messengers were hurled to the earth.

10-12 Then I heard a loud voice in heaven saying: "Just now have come salvation and power and the kingdom realm of our God, and the authority of his Anointed One. Because the accuser of our fellow believers, who accuses them in front of our God day and night has been hurled down. *11* And they conquered him by the Blood of the Lamb and by the Message of their testimony. They were willing to give up their lives. *12* For this reason rejoice, you heavenly places and those who encamp in them. But alas for the earth and the sea, because Slanderer-Liar has gone down to you! He is in a major rage, because he knows the time is short!"

13-18 And when the dragon realized that it had been hurled to the earth, it chased the woman who had given birth to the male child.

14 The woman was given the two wings of a huge eagle, so that she could fly to the place prepared for her in the desert. In that place she would be taken care of for a time, times, and half a time. *15* And the snake spat out water like a river from its mouth, in order to overtake the woman and sweep her away in the current. *16* The earth helped the woman by swallowing the river that the dragon had spat out of its mouth. *17* The dragon was furious with the woman and went off to make war against the rest of her offspring - those who obey God's commandments and hold onto to Jesus' testimony. *18* And the dragon stood on the seashore.

Azazel is one of the main Fallen Angels, one of the Watchers. The name "Azazel" is mistranslated "scapegoat" by several Bible versions, a mistranslation started by Tyndale's 16th century English translation and followed by such versions as the *King James Version*, and the *New International Version*. It is translated correctly as "Azazel" in the *Revised Standard Version* and the *English Standard Version*. Tyndale misread the Hebrew word to mean "escaped goat" and coined the word "scapegoat."

The name Azazel occurs three times in the Old Testament /Hebrew Bible, in Leviticus 16: 8, 10, 26. The context is that on *Yom Kippur,* the Day of Atonement, the high priest performed the set sacrifices for himself and his family then presented the victims for the sins of the people. These were a ram for the burnt offering, and two young goats for the sin-offering. The high priest brought the goats before Yahweh at the door of the tabernacle, and cast lots for them, one lot "for Yahweh" and the other lot "for Azazel." The goat that fell by lot to Yahweh was killed as a sin-offering for the people. The high priest laid his hands on the head of the goat that fell by lot to Azazel and confessed the sins of the people over it. The goat was then handed over to a man who led it to an isolated region and let it go in the wilderness.

Leviticus 16:6: "Aaron will offer the bull as a sin offering for himself and shall make atonement for himself and for his family. *7* Then he will take the two goats and set them before the Lord at the entrance of the tent of meeting. *8* And Aaron will cast lots over the two goats, one lot for the Lord and the other lot for Azazel. *9* And Aaron will present the goat on which the lot fell for the Lord and use it as a sin offering, *10* but the goat on which the lot fell for Azazel will be presented alive before the Lord to make atonement over it, and it will be sent away into the wilderness to Azazel. ..... *26* And he who lets the goat go to Azazel will wash his clothes and bathe his body in water, and then afterwards he may come back into the camp."

The 13th century Nahmanides' (Rabbi Moses ben Nachman's) commentary on Leviticus 26:8 states that Azazel belongs to the class of *se'irim*, hairy goat like demons. This follows Rabbi Abraham ibn Ezra's commentary although ibn Ezra did not state this explicitly. Isaiah 34:15 states, "The wild animals of the desert will meet with the howlers, and the hairy goat demon (*se'irim*) will cry to its fellow. Lilith will settle there and find for herself a resting place." Isaiah 13:21 states, "But the desert dwellers will recline there, and their dwellings will be full of howling creatures, and female unclean birds[36] will live there, and hairy goat demons (*se'irim*) will dance there."

2 Chronicles 11:15 states, "And he appointed his own priests for the high places, and for the hairy goat demons (*se'irim*), and for the calf idols which he had made."

The *Septuagint* (ancient Greek translation of the Hebrew Scriptures), translates *se'irim* by an ancient Greek word meaning "profane" or "useless."

In the first to second century Jewish text[37] the *Apocalypse of Abraham*, Azazel is portrayed as an unclean bird which came down upon the sacrifice prepared by Abraham.[38] It describes Azazel as an evil spirit, a liar, and as an entity that brings troubles to humans who live wickedly.[39] The *Apocalypse of Abraham* states that the wicked will decay in the belly of the cunning worm Azazel, and be burned by the fire of Azazel's tongue."[40] Azazel's appearance is described as a dragon with hands and feet like a human's, and having six wings on the right and six wings on the left of his back."[41] God is said to share the earth with Azazel.[42]

Islam tradition holds Azazel as one of the Jinn. Jinn (or Djinn) are Arabian spiritual beings who are shape shifters, evil spirits, and treacherous spirits who can create illusions. They are creatures of flame and were created from smokeless fire and the searing wind. There are many different kinds of Jinn. Jinn are considered to be the cause of shooting stars, whirlwinds, and sandstorms. They prefer to live in desolate places.

In Islamic tradition, Azazel is identified with Iblis (Eblis).[43] The Qur'an states that when the angels were told to submit to Adam they did, but Iblis refused and was arrogant.[44] It also states that Iblis said Allah created him out of fire while humans were created out of clay, and that Allah banished him.[45]

This is an excerpt from the Islamic *Twenty-first Discourse On Addressing Iblis the Accursed*: "The Shaikh (may Allah be well pleased with him, and may He grant him contentment) said: I saw Iblis in a dream, where I was in the midst of a big crowd. I was on the point of killing him, when he said to me (may Allah curse him): 'Why are you going to kill me? What is my offense? If evil is entailed by destiny, I am powerless to change it and transform it into good, and if good is so entailed I cannot change it and transform it into evil. So what do I control?'

"Hermaphroditic in appearance, he was soft-spoken, with distorted features, wisps of hair on his chin, misshapen and deformed. When he smiled at me, the smile was bashful and apprehensive.

"This happened on the night of Sunday, 12th of Dhu'l-Hijja in the year 516 [of the Hijra].

"Allah is the Guide to all that is good!"[46]

***1 Enoch* 12:1-6.**

Before all these things, Enoch was hidden, and none of the humans knew where he was hidden, where he had been, and what had happened. His days were with the sacred ones, and his doings were to do with the Watchers.

I, Enoch, was blessing the great Lord and King of ages, when the Watchers called me - Enoch the scribe - and said to me, "Enoch, you just scribe of justice, go and tell the Watchers of heaven, who have deserted the high heaven, the sacred everlasting place, who have been defiled with women and have done as the humans do, by taking wives for themselves, 'You have greatly caused corruption on the earth. You will never have peace or forgiveness for your crimes. You will have no delight in your offspring, for you will see the slaughter of their loved ones, and you will lament for the destruction of your children. You can make petition forever, but you will not obtain compassion or peace!"

13:1-10.

Then Enoch went on and said to Azazel, "You will not find peace. A severe sentence has gone out against you, that you are to be bound. You will find no relief, compassion, or granting of requests, because of the injustice you have taught, because of every act of blasphemy, lawlessness, and wrongdoing, which you have shown to humankind."

Then I left him and spoke to them all together, and they were terrified, seized with fear and trembling. They asked me to write a petition for them so that they might find forgiveness, and for me to read their petition in the presence of the Lord of heaven, because from then on they could not address him, or lift up their eyes to heaven on account of the appalling offence for which they were judged.

Then I wrote out their petition and the prayer for their spirits, for everything which they had done, and in regard to their requests, that they should have forgiveness and rest. Then I continued on and sat down at the waters of Dan, in the land of Dan, to the right of the west of Hermon. I read their petition until I fell asleep.

And a dream came to me, and visions fell on me. I saw visions of punishment, so that I might relate it to the heavenly ones, and reprimand them. When I awoke I went to them. They were all sitting gathered together in Abelsjail, which is situated between Lebanon and Seneser,[47] crying, with their faces covered. I related in their presence all the visions which I had seen, and my dream. And I began to utter the just words of justice, reprimanding the heavenly Watchers.

1 Enoch 14:1-25.

This is the book of the just words, and of the reprimand of the Watchers, who are from eternity, according to what the sacred and great one commanded in the vision. I saw in my dream, what I will now speak with a tongue of flesh, and my breath, which the Mighty One has given to the human mouth to converse with and to understand with the heart. As he has created and given to humans the power of comprehending the word of understanding, so has he created and given to me the power of reprimanding the Watchers, the heavenly ones.

"I have written your petition, and in my vision it appeared to me, that what you request will not be granted to you as long as the world lasts. Judgment has been passed on you: your request will not be granted to you. From this time forward, you will not ascend into heaven for all eternity, and he has said that you will be bound on the earth as long as the world lasts. And before these things, you will see the destruction of your loved offspring. You will not have them, but they will fall in front of you by the sword. Your petition on their behalf will not be granted, nor for yourselves, despite your crying and praying and speaking all the words in the writing which I have written."

1 Enoch 15:1-12.

Then he answered me, and I heard his voice. He said, "Don't be afraid, Enoch, you are a just scribe of justice. Approach, and hear my voice. Go, and say to the heavenly Watchers, who have sent you to pray for them, 'You ought to pray for humans, and not humans for you. You have left the high and sacred heaven, which lasts for ever, and have slept with women. You have defiled yourselves with the human women and have taken wives, you have acted like the humans, and you have produced Nephilim as your offspring!

"And although you were sacred, spiritual, and possessing

eternal life, you have defiled yourselves with the blood of women, have produced with the blood of the natural realm, have lusted like humans and have done as those who are flesh and blood do. These however die and perish. Therefore have I given them wives, that they might get them pregnant and produce children with them, and that this might be conducted on the earth. But you from the beginning were made spiritual, having eternal life, immortal for all generations. Therefore I did not make wives for you, because, being spiritual, your dwelling is in heaven.

"Now the Nephilim, who are produced from spirit and flesh, will be called on earth evil spirits, and they will live on earth. Evil spirits have proceeded from their bodies, because they were created from humans: from the sacred Watchers was their beginning and primary origin. Evil spirits they will be on earth, and the spirits of the wicked they will be called.

"As for the spirits of heaven, they will live in heaven, but as for the spirits of the earth which were born on the earth, they will live on the earth. The spirits of the Nephilim will oppress, afflict, destroy, do battle, and bruise on the earth. They will cause grief. They will not eat food, and they will be thirsty, they will cause trouble. They will[48] rise up against the humans, and against women, because they have proceeded from them."

18:1-16.

I then saw the holders of all the winds. I saw how they contributed to the whole creation and the foundations of the earth. I saw the cornerstone of the earth. I also saw the four winds, which bear up the earth, and the structure of the sky. And I saw the winds occupying the high sky, being in the midst of heaven and of earth, and constituting the pillars of heaven.

I saw the winds of the sky, which turn and cause the orb of the sun and of all the stars to set, and over the earth I saw the winds carrying the clouds. I saw the paths of the angels. I saw the structure of the sky above at the extremity of the earth. Then I headed south, and saw a place which burns day and night, where there are seven mountains formed of superb stones, three towards the east, and three towards the south. Of those which were towards the east, one was a colored stone; one was of pearl, and another of healing stone.

Those towards the south were of a red stone.

The middle one reached to heaven like God's throne. It was of alabaster, and the top was of sapphire. I also saw blazing fire. Over all the mountains is a place on the other side of a large territory, where waters were collected. I also saw a deep abyss, with columns of heavenly fire. And in the heavenly columns I saw fires, which were beyond measure both as regards their height and depth. Over this abyss I also saw a place which did not have the structure of the sky above it, nor the solid ground underneath it. There was no water above it, nor any birds, but it was a desolate place. And there I saw seven stars, like great blazing mountains, and like spirits entreating me.

There I saw seven stars like great burning mountains, and when I inquired about them, the angel said, "This place is the end of heaven and earth: this has become a prison for the stars and the host of heaven. The stars which roll over the fire are those which disobeyed the Lord's instruction in the beginning of their time, because they did not come at their appointed times. Therefore he was angry with them, and bound them until the time when their sentence would be completed, in ten thousand years."

19:1-3.

Then Uriel said to me, "The angels who were promiscuous with women will stand here. Their spirits will assume many different forms. They will defile humankind and lead them astray into sacrificing to demons as gods. They will stand here until the great day of judgment, in which they will be judged, until they are made an end of. But their wives who led astray the angels of heaven will find peace."

And I, Enoch, alone saw the vision of the end of all things. No other human saw what I saw.

The Books of Enoch mention other Fallen Angels. Araqiel is named as one of the fallen Watchers in the First Book of Enoch. He taught humans the signs of the earth. The Third Book of Enoch says that Baraqijal (alternate spellings: Baraqiel, Baraqel, Barakiel, Barkiel) was the angel of lightning and is appointed over the second heaven. Baraqiel is named in the First Book of Enoch as one of the

Watchers who was a leader of a group of Ten Watchers, and was also one of the fallen Watchers. 1 Enoch states that Baraqijal taught humans astrology.

The First Book of Enoch says that the Watcher Ezeqeel was one of the Fallen Angels, and that he taught people the knowledge of the clouds. Kokaqbiel (alternate spellings Kokbiel, Kokabiel, Kokabel) is named in the First Book of Enoch as one of the Watchers who was a leader of a group of Ten Watchers, and was also one of the fallen Watchers. 1 Enoch states that Kokaqbiel taught humans the constellations and is appointed over the planets:

"There are seven princes, the great, beautiful, respected, wonderful and honored ones who are appointed over the seven heavens. These are their names: Michael, Gabriel, Shatquiel, Baradiel, Shachaqiel, Baraqiel and Sidril..... Under them is Kokbiel, the prince who is appointed over all the planets. With him are 365,000 multitudes of ministering angels, great and honored ones who move the planets from city to city and from province to province in the Raqia of heavens. Over them are 72 princes of kingdoms on high corresponding to the 72 languages of the world. All of them are crowned with royal crowns, dressed in royal clothes, and wrapped in royal cloaks. All of them are riding royal horses and are holding royal scepters in their hands. And when he is traveling in Raqia, before each one of them royal servants are running with great splendor and magnificence, and in front of every one of them when traveling in Raqia, there are great armies, such as is the custom on earth, with great splendid chariots, and praise, song, and honor."

Matariel (under alternate spelling Armaros) is named in the First Book of Enoch as one of the Watchers who was a leader of a group of Ten Watchers, and was also one of the fallen Watchers.

Sariel is one of the two angels (the other being Raguel) who escorted Enoch through the heavens in the Second Book of Enoch. Sariel is named in the First Book of Enoch as one of the leaders of the fallen Watchers. He taught humans the course of the moon.

Semjaza was named in the First Book of Enoch as the leader of the fallen Watchers. He taught spell potions and rootwork. Other spellings of the name include Samyaza, Semiaza, Samjaza, Shemhazai, Shemyazaz, and Semihazah.

The First Book of Enoch 6:1-8 says, "It happened after the humans had multiplied, that in those times daughters were born to them, and they were attractive and beautiful. When the angels, the inhabitants of heaven, saw them, they lusted after them and said to each other, 'Come on, let's choose consorts for ourselves from the humans, and let's produce children!'

"Then their leader Semjaza said to them, 'I'm concerned as I fear that perhaps you won't agree to carry out this venture, and that I alone will have to pay the penalty for such a serious crime.'

"But they answered, 'Let's all swear an oath, and bind ourselves by mutual curses, that we will not change our minds but carry through this venture.'

"So they swore all together and bound themselves by mutual curses. They were two hundred in number, they descended in the time of Jared, on the top of Mount Hermon. They called it Mount Hermon because they had sworn an oath on it and bound themselves by mutual curses."

An Aramaic text reads "Watchers," instead of the word "angels" above.

The Third Book of Enoch says Zaqiel is appointed over the sparks and in fact is the Angel of Sparks. Alternate spellings of Zaqiel's name are Ziqiel, Zeqiel. Zaqiel is named in the First Book of Enoch as one of the Watchers who was a leader of a group of Ten Watchers, and was also one of the fallen Watchers.

The First Book of Enoch says that Asbeel was the one who suggested an evil plan to the Watchers, and caused them to have sex with the human women.

Chapter 6. The Watchers who did not Fall

1 Enoch 20:1-8 mentions certain Watchers who did not "fall." "These are the names of the sacred angels who watch: Uriel, one of the sacred angels, who presides over the world and Tartarus; Raphael, one of the sacred angels, who is over human spirits; Raguel, one of the sacred angels, who inflicts punishment on the world and the luminaries; Michael, one of the sacred angels who is over the most part of humankind, in charge of the nations; Saraqael, one of the sacred angels, who presides over the spirits of the humans that do wrong; Gabriel, one of the sacred angels, who presides over the seraphim,[49] over paradise,[50] and over the cherubim; Remiel, one of the sacred angels, whom God set over those who rise."

Of those Watchers mentioned above by 1 Enoch, Uriel, Michael, Gabriel, and Raphael also figure in the *Testament of Solomon*, an Old Testament pseudepigraphical work, said to be, as the name suggests, written by King Solomon. It describes how Solomon was able to build the Temple by commanding demons, thanks to a ring given to him by the archangel Michael.

Raphael, Gabriel, Uriel and Michael are all mentioned in *The Testament of Solomon*. The Testament of Solomon is an Old Testament pseudepigraphical work, said to be, as the name suggests, written by King Solomon. It describes how Solomon was able to build the Temple by commanding demons, thanks to a ring given to him by the archangel Michael.

When a demon named Ornias harasses a servant, who happens to be a favorite of Solomon's, by stealing half his pay and sucking out his life-force through the servant's thumb, Solomon prays for help. As a result, the archangel Michael gives him a ring with the seal of God on it. The ring gives him the power to command demons. Solomon gives the ring to the servant and tells him to throw it at the demon Ornias's chest while ordering Ornias to go to Solomon.

Ornias tells Solomon he is the offspring of the archangel Uriel. Solomon had trouble with Ornias, so prayed that the archangel Uriel would come and help him. Uriel came from heaven and made the sea monsters come out of the deep. Uriel told the demon Ornias to cut the stones for the Temple. Solomon ordered the demon Ornias to take the ring and do the same thing to Beelzebub, the prince of demons. Beelzebub says he used to be the highest ranking angel in Heaven.

Solomon questions all the demons as to which angel can frustrate them. The demon Error and the demon Artosael are frustrated by Uriel. The demon Ruaz is frustrated by Michael. The demon Barsafael is frustrated by Gabriel. The demon Asmodeus and the demon the demon Obizuth are frustrated by Raphael. Solomon eventually has control over all the demons and gets them to build the Temple.

Raguel and Sariel were the two angels who led Enoch through the heavens in 2 Enoch. Raguel is named in 1 Enoch 20 as one of the Watchers who did not fall. "Raguel, one of the sacred angels, who inflicts punishment on the world and the luminaries."

The Book of Daniel (4:17) in the Hebrew Bible / Old Testament mentions a "Watcher." Nebuchadnezzar tells Daniel that he saw in a vision or dream a "sacred Watcher" who appeared to him and made an announcement. In the vision the Watcher concluded, "This announcement is by the decree of the Watchers, this command is by the word of the sacred ones, so that those who are alive may understand that the Supreme has authority over the human kingdoms, and he gives it to whomever he wishes. He sets up even the lowest ranked human beings over them." (From *The Source Bible*.) The *Septuagint* (Greek Old Testament) translates the word for "Watcher" as "angel." However, Theodotion (c. 200 A.D.), the Jewish scholar who made a translation of the Hebrew Bible into Greek, transliterates the word. That is, he simply put it into Greek letters without attempting to translate it, as one does with names.

Gabriel is a well known angel and 1 Enoch puts him into the Watcher category. The Third Book of Enoch says that the archangel Gabriel, the prince of the host, is appointed over the sixth heaven. and names him as the angel of the fire.

In Islam, Gabriel revealed the Qur'an to Mohammed, and is the angel who communicates with all the prophets.

Here are the major ancient sources on Gabriel.

Luke Chapter 1 (New Testament)

5-7 In the time of Herod, the king of Judea, there was a certain priest named Zacharias. He was a member of the priestly order of Abijah. His wife was one of the descendants of Aaron, and her name was Elizabeth. *6* They were both right before God, and they acted blamelessly as to all the commandments and regulations of the Lord. *7* But they didn't have any children, as Elizabeth was barren and they were both getting on in years.

8-11 Now it turned out that while Zacharias was serving God with his priestly duties when his priestly division was on duty, he was chosen by lot – *9* this was in line with the priestly custom - to burn incense when he went into the temple of the Lord. *10* At the time of the incense offering, the whole crowd of people was praying outside. *11* An angel of the Lord appeared in front of him, standing on the right side of the incense altar.

12-17 When Zacharias saw him, he got all mixed up and he became quite scared. *13* But the angel reassured him, "Zacharias, don't be afraid! Your earnest request has been heard. Your wife Elizabeth will bear you a son, and you must give him the name 'John'. *14* He will be a joy and a delight to you, and lots of people will shout joyfully because of him. *15* He will be important in the Lord's sight! He'll never take wine or sweet fermented liquor and he will be filled with the Holy Spirit even from birth. *16* He will bring back many Israelites to the Lord their God. *17* He will go on ahead of the Lord to prepare people for the Lord. He will be equipped with the same spirit and power that Elijah had, to correct the attitudes of parents to their children. He will correct disobedient people so that they will have the common sense of the people who are right with God, and make ready for the Lord people who are well prepared for him."

18-20 "What's going to make me believe that this is the case! Zacharias asked the angel. "Me - I'm an old man, that's for sure, and my wife's well and truly getting on years!"

19 The angel answered, "I am Gabriel, who stands in the presence of God, and who was sent to announce this Good News to you! *20* Well then! You will be silent! As you didn't believe my words, which will in fact turn out just as I said, you won't be able to speak a word until the very day it actually happens!"

21-23 The people waited for Zacharias. They were surprised that he was spending such a long time in the temple. *22* When he came out, he couldn't speak to them. They realized that he had seen a vision, because he kept on making signs and stayed firmly speechless the whole time. *23* And it turned out that as soon as his time of priestly ministry was completed, he went back home.

24-25 After these events his wife Elizabeth became pregnant and lived in seclusion for five months. *25* "The Lord has done this for me!" she exclaimed. "He was watching over me to take away my inability to have children which the people considered to be a disgrace."

26-29 When Elizabeth was six months pregnant, God sent the angel Gabriel to Nazareth, a city in Galilee, *27* to an unmarried girl who was engaged to a man named Joseph, a descendant of David. The unmarried girl's name was Mary. *28* The angel greeted her, "Hello there, you highly favored person! The Lord is with you!" *29* But she was deeply disturbed and wondered what sort of greeting this was!

30-38 The angel continued, "Don't be afraid, Mary! You've found favor with God! *31* You will become pregnant and give birth to a son, and you are to name him Jesus. *32* He will be very important, and will be called the Son of the Most High, and the Lord God will give him the throne of his ancestor David. *33* He will reign over the house of Jacob forever, and his Realm will never end."

34 "How can this be?" Mary asked the angel. "I'm a virgin: I haven't been with a man!"

35 The angel answered, "The Holy Spirit will come upon you and the power of the Most High will spread his shadow over you. The one to be born will be sacred and will be called the Son of God. *36* Your relative Elizabeth has also become pregnant with a son in her old age. They said she was unable to have children but now she is six months pregnant! *37* Every spoken word from God has power!"

38 "Fantastic!" Mary exclaimed. "I am the Lord's slave servant! May everything you've said come true!" And then the angel left her.

This is what the Old Testament / Hebrew Bible says about Gabriel.

Daniel 8:15-27

Then it came about that when I, Daniel, had seen the vision and was looking for its meaning, that suddenly someone who looked like a human stood in front of me. I heard a human voice calling out from the Ulai river banks, "Gabriel, tell this man the meaning of the vision."

So he approached the place where I was standing and then I became terrified and I fell on my face. He said to me, "Human, understand that the events you have seen in your vision relate to the future."

Now, as he was speaking with me, I was in a deep sleep with my face to the ground, but he touched me, and stood me upright. He said, "I'm here to reveal to you what will happen later in angry times. What you have seen pertains to the very end of time. The two-horned ram you saw represents the kings of Media and Persia. The hairy goat demon you saw is the king of Ionia, and the large horn between its eyes is the first king. As for the horn that was broken, and the four others that took its place, four kingdoms will rise from that nation, but not by his power. And at the end time of their kingdom, when the wrongdoers have reached their limit, a king of bold appearance, one who understands enigmas, will arise. He will be very powerful but not by his own power. He will cause a huge amount of destruction and everything he does will succeed. He will destroy powerful leaders and devastate the sacred people. He will cunningly make deceitfulness prosper by his power, and he will praise himself. He will carelessly destroy many. He will rise up against the Leader of leaders, but in the end his power will be broken. The vision of the evening and morning that has been told to you is true, but hide the vision, as it's about the distant future."

"And I, Daniel, was weak for several days. Afterwards I got up and attended to the king's business, but I was appalled by the vision and no one understood it."

Daniel 9:21-27

While I was praying, the one Gabriel, whom I had seen in the vision at the beginning, ran swiftly, and approached me about the time of the evening offering.

He explained to me, "Daniel, I've come here to give you insight and understanding. At the beginning of your prayers the word went out, and I've come to report it to you, for you are loved. So discern the utterance and understand the vision. Seventy weeks are marked out for your people and your sacred city, to stop rebellion, to put wrongdoing to an end, to make atonement for crime, to bring in continual justice, and to hide the vision and prophecy, and to anoint the most sacred.

"So perceive and understand that from the going out of the word to restore and build Jerusalem to the coming of the anointed one, a prince, there will be seven weeks. Then for sixty-two weeks it will be built again with streets and moat, but in a time of distress. After the sixty-two weeks, the anointed one will be cut off and will have nothing. The people of the leader who is to come will destroy the city and the sanctuary. Its end will come with a flood, and devastations are decreed up to the end of the war. And he will cut a covenant with many for one week, and for half the week he will make the sacrifice and offering cease. He will devastate the edges of the detestable, until that which is decided is poured out on the devastator."

Michael is a powerful archangel who is named as a Watcher by 1 Enoch. Michael appears frequently in ancient texts. The Third Book of Enoch says, "Michael, the great prince, is appointed over the seventh heaven, the highest one, which is in the Araboth." In Islam, Michael is the archangel of mercy who brings rain and thunder to the earth. He also makes sure rewards are handed out to those who do good, and provides nourishment.

Here are the instances of Michael in the New Testament.
Jude 9
But Michael the Archangel, when he was deciding the dispute, discoursing with Slanderer-Liar about Moses' body, did not dare to impose an abusive sentence on him, but said, "May the Lord impose the penalty on you!"
Revelation 12,
7-9 War broke out in heaven. Michael and his angel waged war against the dragon, and the dragon and his angels fought back. *8* But the dragon wasn't strong enough, and thus they no longer had a place in heaven. *9* The mighty dragon was thrown down - that ancient snake called "Slanderer-Liar", and also called "Adversary," who leads the whole earth astray. He and his angels were hurled to the earth.

Here are the instances of Michael in the Old Testament / Hebrew Bible.

Daniel 10:2-21

In those days I, Daniel, was mourning for three weeks. I did not eat any tasty food, no meat or wine touched my lips, and I did not use any lotions at all until the three weeks were over. On the twenty-fourth day of the first month, as I was standing on the bank of the great river, the Tigris, I looked up and there in front of me was a man dressed in linen, and wearing a belt of fine gold from Uphaz around his waist.

His body was like a precious yellow gemstone, his face shone like lightning, his eyes were like fiery torches, his arms and legs gleamed like burnished bronze, and his voice sounded like a crowd of people speaking.

I, Daniel, was the only one who saw the vision. The people with me did not see it, but such fear came on them that they fled and hid themselves. So I was left alone and saw this great vision. No strength was left in me. My vigor was completely destroyed and I had no strength at all. Then I heard the sound of his words, and when I heard the sound of his words, I was on my face in a deep sleep with my face to the ground. A hand touched me which shook me to my knees and on the palms of my hands!

He said to me, "Daniel, you greatly loved person, discern the words I'm about to tell you, and stand up! I have now been sent to you."

When he said this to me, I stood up shuddering. Then he said to me, "Don't be afraid, Daniel. Since the first day you began to pray for understanding and to be occupied with Elohim's presence, your words were heard, and I've come because of your words. But the spirit leader of the kingdom of Persia withstood me for twenty-one days, but Michael, one of the foremost spirit leaders, came to help me, as I was left there with the spirit kings of Persia. Now I've come to explain to you what will happen to your people in the future, for the vision concerns a time yet to come. Now I've come so you will discern what will happen to your people in the future, as the vision is about the future."

When he said this to me, I bowed with my face toward the ground and I was unable to speak. Then the one who looked like a human touched my lips, and I opened my mouth and spoke. I said to the one standing in front of me, "I'm utterly distressed by the vision, and my strength has left me! How can someone like me, your master's servant, talk to you, my master? I have no strength left, and I can hardly breathe."

Then the one who looked like a human touched me again and gave me strength. He said, "Don't be afraid, you loved person. Be at peace, be strong, be strong!"

As he spoke these words, I suddenly grew stronger and said to him, "Now please speak, my master, you've strengthened me."

He replied, "Do you know why I've come? Soon I have to return to fight against the spirit prince of the kingdom of Persia, and then when I have left, the spirit leader of the kingdom of Ionia will come! But I will tell you what is written in the truthful writings, and there is no one who supports me against these except Michael, your spirit leader."

Daniel 12:1

"At that time Michael, the great spirit leader who takes a stand for your people, will take a stand. There will be a time of trouble such as has not happened from the beginning of nations until then. But at that time your people - those whose names are found written in the book - will escape."

The Archangel Raphael is associated especially with healing. In ancient Greek a certain word was used for divine healing by God. In the *Septuagint*, this word is also used for Raphael's healing of others. The word is reserved for Raphael and God.

Raphael and Uriel are not mentioned in the Old Testament / Hebrew Bible or the New Testament. Raphael features strongly in the *Book of Tobit*, a book of scripture that is part of the Catholic and Orthodox Biblical canon, and found in the *Septuagint,* which is quoted in the New Testament. It was widely used by the Hellenistic Jews of the era.

Hebrew and Aramaic fragments of the *Book of Tobit* were discovered in Cave IV at Qumran in 1952. The *Book of Tobit* was put forward by the Council of Carthage of 397 and confirmed for Roman Catholics in 1546 by the Council of Trent. Tobit is considered apocryphal by Protestants, and was not included as canon by ancient Judaism.

In the *Book of Tobit*, Raphael tells Tobit that God sent him to cure his blindness and to help his daughter-in-law Sara as the evil spirit Asmodeus had killed her 7 husbands. The *Book of Tobit* 3:17 states, "Raphael was sent to heal them both, that is, to scale away the whiteness of Tobit's eyes, and to give Sara the daughter of Raguel as a wife to Tobias, Tobit's son, and to bind the evil spirit Asmodeus."

The *Book of Tobit* 12:15 states, "I am Raphael, one of the seven sacred angels who present the prayers of the people devoted to God, and I go in and out in the presence of the splendor of the Sacred One."

In the *Book of Tobit*, Raphael tells Tobit that God sent him to cure his blindness and to help his daughter-in-law Sara as the evil spirit Asmodeus had killed her 7 husbands. The *Book of Tobit* 3:17 states, "Raphael was sent to heal them both, that is, to scale away the whiteness of Tobit's eyes, and to give Sara the daughter of Raguel as a wife to Tobias, Tobit's son, and to bind the evil spirit Asmodeus."

Hoodoo tradition says that one can take three bay leaves and write the names of Michael, Gabriel, and Raphael on ink on each leaf, then tie these leaves in white cloth and carry them to ensure success in sports contests. Uriel was not mentioned.

Uriel (Uri + El) in Hebrew means "Light of El" or "Illumination /Revelation of El." (Remember that El is one of the names of the Hebrew God.) The first part of his name Uri refers mainly to light in general, but can also refer to the light from a flame. It also can mean "revelation." There is very interesting connection here. The Urim were very mysterious things that the ancient High Priest of the Hebrews used for divination. To this day, no one really knows what they were. They were used along with the Thummim by the High Priest to find out God's will. Joshua and his successors were only able to speak to Yahweh through the High Priest by means of the Urim and Thummim.

Here is the account of Uriel in 1 Enoch 80:1-8.

In those days Uriel answered me, "I have showed you everything, Enoch, and I have revealed everything to you. You see the sun, the moon, and the leaders of the stars of heaven, which cause all their operations, seasons, and departures. The years will be shortened in the times of wrongdoers. Their offspring will be backward in their prolific soil, and everything done on earth will be subverted, and will not appear in its season. The rain will be held back, and heaven will withhold it. In those days the fruits of the earth will be late, and will not flourish at their proper time, and in their season the fruits of the trees will be withheld at their proper time.

"The moon will change its laws, and not be seen at its proper time. But in those days it will be seen in heaven, on top of a great chariot in the west. It will shine more than light should shine. Many leaders of the stars will wander off, change their ways and actions. Those will not appear at their proper times which have been prescribed for them, and all the classes of the stars will be shut up against wrongdoers. The thoughts of the inhabitants of the earth will go astray concerning them, and they will go astray from their ways. They will do wrong, and think themselves gods, and evil will increase among them. Punishment will come on them and destroy them."

Chapter 7. Nephilim and Giants.

The Nephilim were the offspring of the Watchers and humans. The First Book of Enoch tells what happened: "It happened after the humans had multiplied, that in those times daughters were born to them, and they were attractive and beautiful. When the angels, the inhabitants of heaven, saw them, they lusted after them and said to each other, 'Come on, let's choose consorts for ourselves from the humans, and let's produce children!'

"Then their leader Semjaza said to them, 'I'm concerned as I fear that perhaps you won't agree to carry out this venture, and that I alone will have to pay the penalty for such a serious crime.'

"But they answered, 'Let's all swear an oath, and bind ourselves by mutual curses, that we will not change our minds but carry through this venture.'

"So they swore all together and bound themselves by mutual curses. They were two hundred in number; they descended in the time of Jared, on the top of Mount Hermon. They called it Mount Hermon because they had sworn an oath on it and bound themselves by mutual curses.

"They and the rest took consorts. Each one chose their own. They had sex with them and defiled themselves with them. They taught them charms and sorceries, the cutting of roots, and the uses of plants.

"The women got pregnant and gave birth to Nephilim whose height was three hundred cubits. They consumed everything humans produced. When humans could no longer sustain them, they turned against them, in order to consume them. They began to do wrong against birds, beasts, reptiles, and fish, and to eat each other's flesh, and to drink their blood. Then the earth laid accusation against the lawless ones."

There is a parallel account in Genesis 6:1-4: "When humankind began to increase on the face of the earth, and daughters were born to them, those associated with Elohim saw that the human women were beautiful and so they took wives for themselves from any they chose. .. The Nephilim were on the earth in those times, and also afterwards, when those associated with Elohim were having sex with the human women, who gave birth to their children. They were the mighty heroes of ancient times, the famous ones."

The word "Nephilim" occurs only twice in the Old Testament /Hebrew Bible, in Genesis 6:4 (see above) and Numbers 13:33. Here is the mention in Numbers 13:33: "And there we saw the Nephilim (the Anakims, who come from the Nephilim), and we seemed to ourselves to be like grasshoppers, and we seemed the same to them."

It is unlikely that the "Nephilim" of Numbers 13:33 were the Nephilim of Genesis 6:4.

Goliath was not a Nephilim. The two passages in Old Testament / Hebrew Bible which mention Nephilim have nothing to do with Goliath.

1 Samuel 17:4 in the Hebrew Bible / Old Testament says, "And a champion went out from the camp of the Philistines. His name was Goliath, and he was from Gath, and his height was six cubits and a span." The *Septuagint*, the *Dead Sea Scrolls,* and *Josephus* have his height as 4 cubits and a span, which is 6 ¾ feet tall (2 metres). Six cubits and span is 9 feet tall. However, Goliath was not called a Nephilim. Note that the *gigas* (which rarely appears in the singular and is the word which translates Nephilim in the *Septuagint*) Alcyoneus was said to be 9 cubits high.[51]

For some reason, the word "Nephilim" is translated by the English word "Giants" in several Bible versions. This may be because Numbers 13:33 states that when they saw the Nephilim, they figured that they would look like locusts to them. Some have interpreted this to mean that the Nephilim towered over them. The word "Rephaim" is also rendered by the English word "giants" in several Bible versions.

Deuteronomy 2:11
Like the Anakims, they too were considered Rephaim, but the Moabites called them Emims.

Deuteronomy **2:20**
That area, too, was once considered to be the land of the Rephaim, and the Ammonites referred to them as Zamzummims.

***2 Samuel* 21:20**
In still another battle, which took place at Gath, there was a man of stature with six fingers on each hand and six toes on each foot, twenty-four in all. He also was descended from the Rephaim.

***Deuteronomy* 3:11**
King Og of Bashan was the last of the Rephaim. His iron bed was more than 9 cubits (13 feet = 4.1 metres) long and 4 cubits (6 feet = 1.8 metres) wide. It remains today in the Ammonite city of Rabbah.

***Deuteronomy* 3:13**
I gave the rest of Gilead and also all of Bashan, the kingdom of Og, to the half tribe of Manasseh. The whole region of Argob in Bashan used to be known as a land of the Rephaim.

Note that Goliath is often said to be one of the Nephilim, but there is no evidence for this. As we have seen, the two passages in Old Testament / Hebrew Bible which mention Nephilim have nothing to do with Goliath.

***1 Samuel* 17:4.**
"And a champion went out from the camp of the Philistines. He name was Goliath, and he was from Gath, and his height was six cubits and a span."

The *Septuagint*, the *Dead Sea Scrolls,* and *Josephus* have Goliath's height as 4 cubits and a span, which is 6 ¾ feet tall (2 metres). Six cubits and span is 9 feet tall. However, Goliath was not called a Nephilim.

"Nephilim" is translated in the *Septuagint* by the word *gigantes*, from which we get our English word "giants," but to the Greeks the "Giants" were a race of supernatural beings that had been destroyed by the Olympian gods, and interestingly, like the fathers of the Nephilim, the "Giants" were also thrown into Tartarus. In later ancient Greek and early Roman times, the "Giants" were confused with the "Titans" who were also destroyed by the Olympian gods. The third century BCE dramatist and epic poet Gnaeus Naevius' poem on the Punic Wars wrongly describes the Giants Runcus and Purpureus as "Titans."[52] Purpureus is the Latin translation of the Greek name Porphyrion, one of the Giants killed by Herakles.

Herakles also killed the Giants Alcyoneus, Damysos, Ephialtes, Leon, Peloreus and Theodamas. Note that Herakles is often written as "Hercules" in English under influence of the Latin spelling.

Josephus states, "For many angels of God had sex with women, and fathered wanton children who disdained everything that was nice, due to the confidence they had in their own power. The tradition handed down is that that these dared to do similar acts to those called Giants by the Greeks. Noah was unable to endure their accomplishments and wanted to persuade them to change their minds and do better, However, as he could not change their minds, and seeing that they would not yield to him, but were stubborn and enjoyed being powerful, he was afraid they would kill him, along with his wife and children, and those with whom they were living, so he emigrated from that land."[53]

In Greek mythology, the Giants were the children of Gaia (Earth), their father being her son Ouranos. Gaia gave birth to eighteen children:

3 Giants - Cottus, Briareus and Gyges. They were huge and very strong. They are sometimes called *Hekatonkheires* ("hundred handed") as they had 100 hands and 50 heads.

3 Cyclopes - Brontes, Sterops and Arges. Each only one eye in the center of their forehead, and they were huge and strong.

12 Titans - 6 male and 6 female. The females were:
Thea - goddess of the light of the *aither* (the air above the direct dome of the earth) - mother of Selene (Moon), Eos (Dawn) and Helios (Sun).
Rhea - earth goddess - mother of the Olympian gods
Themis - associated with Justice, Order, and sometimes associated with Gaia.
Mnemosyne - goddess of memory and mother of the Muses
Phoebe - goddess of light, later associated with Selene - mother of Leto and Asteria
Tethys - goddess of the ocean, mother of the Oceanids
    The males were:
Oceanus - god of the ocean, mother of the Oceanids
Koios - the father of Leto (the mother of Artemis and Apollo) and Asteria.

Krios - the father of Astraios, Pallas and Perses

Hyperion - god of light - father of Selene (Moon), Eos (Dawn) and Helios (Sun).

Iapetos - the father of Prometheus, Atlas, Epimetheus, and Menoetius.

Kronos - the youngest of the Titans, who followed his mother Gaia's plan to attack Ouranos ("Uranus" in Latin). He was a prolific father - Demeter, Hestia, Hera, Hades, Poseidon, Zeus, all from Rhea, and from other mothers, Khiron, Pikos, Aphros and the Korybantes.

After the birth of his children, Ouranos became afraid of their power. Every time Gaia gave birth, Ouranos threw the baby back into Gaia's womb. Gaia devised a plan to castrate Ouranos, but only Kronos agreed to help. Gaia gave Kronos a jagged sickle. Kronos hid and waited for his father to arrive. When Ouranos came by night, Kronos struck. He cut off his father's genitals and threw them into the sea. The genitals covered with blood sprayed over Gaia. Consequently, more children were produced by the blood:

The Furies (Erinyes) - Alecto, Tisiphone, and Megara.[54]

The Giants - Born in full armour and with spears in their arms.

Meliae - Nymphs of the mountain ash trees.[55]

The genitals on the sea produced white foam which in turn produced the goddess Aphrodite.

The Titans made Kronos their king and also freed the Cyclopes and Giants from Tartarus. Kronos later threw the Cyclopes and Giants back into Tartarus. However, twelve Titans were still free. Four pairs of them had children together.

Thea and Hyperion - gave birth to the Helios (Sun), Selene (Moon) and Eos (Dawn)

Phoebe and Koios - gave birth to two daughters - Leto and Asteria

Oceanus and Tethys - gave birth to the Oceanids.

Kronos and Rhea - gave birth to three daughters - Hestia, Demeter, and Hera, and three sons - Hades, Poseidon and Zeus. These became the Olympic gods.

There was a prophecy that Kronos would be overthrown by his own son, so in response he swallowed all his newborn children whole as soon as they were born. Rhea grieved for her lost children.

After she conceived her sixth child, Zeus, Rhea pleaded with her parents Gaia and Ouranos for help. Gaia and Ouranos sent Rhea to Lyktos in Crete. When she gave birth to Zeus, she gave him to Gaia who hid him in a cave in Mount Dicte. Rhea returned to Kronos and gave him a large stone wrapped in baby clothes. Kronos swallowed the stone, thinking it was the baby.

When Zeus grew up, he travelled to the oceans and sought the help of the Oceanid, Metis. Metis gave him an emetic potion to give to Kronos. After Kronos drank the potion, he vomited up all his children as well as the stone.

Zeus and his siblings then went to war with the Titans. This is known today as the *Titanomachy* (War of the Titans) and refers to the war between the new Olympian gods and their predecessors, the Titans.

After ten years, the War of the Titans was in stalemate. Gaia prophesied that Zeus and his siblings could only be victorious if they engaged the help of their uncles, the Giants and the Cyclopes, who were still imprisoned in Tartarus. Zeus went down to Tartarus, killed Kampe the jailer[56] and freed the three Giants and the three Cyclopes.

Kampe was a female serpent or dragon (same word in the ancient Greek language) appointed by Kronos to guard the Giants and Cyclopes when he had them locked in Tartarus. Zeus killed her and freed the Giants from their prison to aide him in his war against the Titans.

Kampe had the body of a woman but was covered in scales from her chest to her thighs. Below that she had the body of a huge snake or dragon and for feet she had a thousand snakes which spat poison a great distance. From her neck sprouted the heads of fifty animals including lions and wild boars. A scorpion's coiled tail rose above her head, and she had poisonous spitting serpents for hair. Two black wings flapped from her shoulders. Her hands were vicious claws. Flames came from her eyelids.[57]

The Cyclopes made new weapons for their rescuers: thunder and lightning for Zeus, a helmet which made its wearer invisible for Hades, and a trident for Poseidon.

Zeus overcame the Titans with the help of the Giants and Cyclopes, and threw them deep in the depths of Tartarus, guarded by the three Giants.

Gaia was upset by the imprisonment of the Titans in Tartarus by the Olympians, so encouraged the Giants to rise up in arms against them, end their reign, and restore the Titans' rule. The Giants led by Alcyoneus and Porphyrion went into battle against the Olympians.

This is known today as the *Gigantomachy* (War of the Giants) and it was a popular theme of Greek vase paintings of the fifth century BCE. Diodorus Siculus describes the depiction of the War if the Giants on the eastern side of the Temple of Olympian Zeus at Akragas.[58] The Temple featured giant statues or columns the shape of male figures (7.61 metres in height) known as Telamons or Atlantes. The Temple possibly dates to 460 BCE.

The massive Altar of Pergamon (now in the Pergamon Museum in Berlin, but originally at Pergamon, as the name suggests) shows in sculptural high relief serpent-legged Giants fighting Olympic gods. The Romans used Pergamon as an administrative center for the province of Asia. Zeus and Athena appear prominently on the frieze. The terminus post quem for the building of the Altar of Pergamon was 172/171 BCE as the foundations contained a pottery shard which was ascribed to that date.

Revelation 2:12-13 states, "And to the Messenger (*angel*) of the assembly of Pergamon write: he who has the sharp, double edged sword says this: I know where you live, that's where the adversary (*satan*) has his throne."

With the assistance of the Moirae (the Fates) and Herakles, the Olympians put down the Giants' rebellion and decisively defeated the Giants. The Olympians called for Herakles' help as the prophecy declared that a non-god was needed to defeat the Giants. Zeus instructed Athena to ask Herakles' assistance in the battle. Herakles came upon the Giant Alcyoneus when he was asleep, and sources differ as to whether he overcame him by an arrow[59] dipped in the poisonous blood of the Hydra or by blows from his club.

The Giant Alcyoneus was immortal so long as he remained in Pallene. Athena advised Herakles to drag Alcyoneus outside Pallene to make the Giant susceptible to death. Once outside Pallene, he was beaten to death by Herakles. Herakles killed not only Alcyoneus, but all the Giants who had been wounded by the Olympians.

The only Giant not killed in the conflict was Aristaios, who was turned into a dung beetle by Gaia to keep him safe from the Olympian gods.

The Olympic gods buried the Giants under the earth, where earthquakes and volcanic activity were caused by their turmoil.

Some of the Giants identified by individual names were:

Alcyoneus - Killed by Herakles.

Porphyrion - Killed by Herakles.

Agrios - Turned into a bird.[60]

Klytius - Killed by Hekate with flaming torches.

Damysos - The speed of his feet was extracted and given to Achilles.

Enceladus - Killed by Athena. The battle of Athena with Enceladus is shown on the west pediment on the Temple of Apollo at Delphi.

Ephialtes - Shot by Apollo and Herakles with arrows.

Eurytus - Killed by Dionysus with his Bacchic wand.

Gration - Killed by the goddess Artemis with her arrows.

Hippolytus - Killed by Hermes with his sword when Hermes was wearing the wearing the cap of Hades which made one invisible.

Leon - Killed by Herakles.

Mimas - According to Apollodorus, Mimas was killed by Hephaestus with masses of red-hot metal. According to Euripides, *Ion*, Mimas was burned to death by Zeus with a thunderbolt, and according to Apollonius Rhodius, *Argonautica*, he was killed by Ares.

Otus of the Aloadae - He and his twin accidentally fatally speared each other.

Pallas - Killed by Athena.

Peloreus.[61]

Polybotes - Crushed by Poseidon beneath the island of Nisyros or Cos.

Theodamas.[62]

Thoon - Clubbed to death by the Fates with clubs of bronze.

Here are more ancient accounts of the Giants.

Virgil, *Aeneid*, 3.578.
A spreading bay is there, unassailable by all assaulting storms, and Mount Etna's mouth with its roaring fearsome thunders is close by. Now it lifts a cloud of pitch black, whirling smoke and burning dust, to the realm of light and spurts out flames with massive tongues that lick the stars. Now its mouth ejects huge crags of itself, ripped out of the depths of the mountain, while the molten rock shoots screaming to the skies. The bottomless abyss causes ebb and flow from the hindmost deep. Enceladus, his body scarred by lightning, lies imprisoned under all, so it is said. Over him massive Etna breathes in fire from crack and seam. If he happens to turn to change his fatigued side, Trinacria's island shudder and groans, and thick fumes layer the skies.

Apollodorus 1.6.1.
Such is the legend of Demeter as it is told, but Gaia, irritated because of the Titans, gave birth to the Giants, whom she had by Ouranos. The size of their bodies was unsurpassed and their strength was invincible. They were terrifying to look at, and had long locks of hair hanging from their head and chin, and had serpent scales for feet.[63] Some say they were born in Phlegrae, but others say they were born in Pallene.[64] They threw rocks and burning oaks at the sky. Exceeding all the rest were Porphyrion and Alcyoneus. Alcyoneus was immortal so long as he fought in the land of his birth. He also drove away the cows of the Sun from Erythia.[65] The gods had an oracle that none of the Giants would be able to be killed by the gods, but that if the gods allied with[66] a mortal they would be able to kill the Giants. After learning this, Gaia looked for a sorcerer to prevent the Giants from being destroyed even by a mortal. However, Zeus forbade the Dawn, the Moon and the Sun to shine, and then Zeus pre-empted it as he himself slaughtered the sorcerer, and then allied himself with Athena and summoned Herakles to help. Herakles first shot Alcyoneus with an arrow, but when the giant fell on the ground he somewhat revived. However, at Athena's advice Herakles dragged him outside Pallene, and so the Giant died.

Pausanias 8.29.1-2

"After crossing the Alpheius you arrive at what is called Trapezuntian territory and the ruins of a city called Trapezus. On the left, as you go down again from Trapezus to the Alpheius, not far from the river there is a place called Depth, where every other year they celebrate the Mysteries to the Great Goddesses. Here there is a spring called Olympias which does not flow every other year, and fire rises up near the spring. The Arcadians say that the legendary battle between Giants and gods took place here and not at Pallene in Thrace,[67] and at this spot sacrifices are offered to lightnings, hurricanes and thunders.

"Homer does not mention Giants at all in the *Iliad*, but in the *Odyssey* he relates how the Laestrygones looking not like humans but Giants attacked Odysseus' ships, and he also has the king of the Phaeacians say that the Phaeacians are similar to the gods like the Cyclopes and the race of Giants. In these places then he indicates that the Giants are mortal and not divine, and his words in the following passage are even clearer: 'Who once was king of the arrogant Giants, but he destroyed the wanton people and he himself was destroyed.' Homer Odyssey 7.59-60. 'Wanton people' in the poetry of Homer means the common people."

Apollodorus 6:2.

In the battle Porphyrion attacked Herakles and Hera, but Zeus put it into Porphyrion's mind to lust after Hera. Porphyrion ripped off her robes and would have forced her, but she called for help. Zeus struck him with a thunderbolt, and Herakles shot him dead with an arrow. As for the remaining giants, Ephialtes was shot by Apollo with an arrow in his left eye and by Herakles in his right eye; Eurytus was killed by Dionysus with a Bacchic wand;[68] Klytius was killed by Hekate with pine-torches, and Mimas was killed by Hephaestus with masses of red-hot metal. Enceladus fled, but Athena threw herself on him as he fled to the island of Sicily, and she skinned Pallas and used his skin to shield her own body in the fight. Polybotes was chased through the sea by Poseidon and arrived at Cos. Poseidon broke off the piece of the island called Nisyros, and threw it on him. Hermes, wearing the helmet of Hades,[69] killed Hippolytus as he was fleeing, and Artemis killed

Gration. The Fates, fighting with bronze war-clubs, killed Agrius and Thoas. Zeus disabled the other Giants by striking them with thunderbolts and Herakles utterly destroyed all of them by shooting them with arrows.

Euripides, *Ion*, 215ff.
[205] I am glancing around everywhere. See the battle of the Giants, on the stone walls.
My friends, I am looking at it.
Do you see the one wielding her gorgon shield against Enceladus?
I see Pallas, my own goddess.
Now what? The mighty thunderbolt, blazing at both ends, in the far-shooting hands of Zeus?
I see it. He is burning the destructive Mimas to ashes with fire.
Bacchic Bacchus is killing another of the Gaia's children with his unwarlike ivy staff.

Apollonius Rhodius, *Argonautica*, 3.1225ff on Minas the Giant.
Then Aeetes put on his chest the firm corslet which Ares had given him when he had killed the Phlegraean Mimas with his own hands.

Strabo, *Geography*, 10.5.16.
Nisyros lies to the north of Telos, and is about sixty stadia[70] away both from it and from Cos. It is round, high and rocky. The rock is that of which millstones are made, and the neighboring people are well supplied with millstones from there. It has also a city of the same name as well as a harbor and hot springs and a Temple of Poseidon. Its perimeter is eighty stadia. The Islands of the Nisyrians are close by. It is said that Nisyros is a section of Cos, and they add the legend that Poseidon, when he was pursuing one of the Giants, Polybotes, broke off a section of Cos with his trident and hurled it upon him, and the part that he threw became an island, Nisyros, with the Giant lying beneath it. However, others say that he lies under Cos.

Pindar, *Pythian*, 8.1-15.

Kindly Serenity, daughter of Justice, you who make cities great, holding the supreme keys of counsel and of wars, please receive this honor due to Aristomenes for his Pythian victory. For you know both how to give and how to receive gentleness, at the very right time. Yet, whenever anyone drives pitiless anger into his heart, you encounter the power of your enemies savagely, sinking Hubris in the flood. Porphyrion did not perceive your power when he roused your anger beyond all measure. Profit is most welcome when one easily takes it from the home of a willing giver. Aggression eventually trips up even a person of great pride. Cilician Typhon with his hundred heads did not escape you, nor certainly did the king of the Giants. One was vanquished by the thunderbolt, and the other by the bow of Apollo, who generously welcomed Xenarces' son when he returned from Cirrha, crowned with a laurel garland from Parnassus and with Dorian victory-song.

Odyssey 7.59, 60.

Odysseus admired the harbors and the regal ships, the meeting-places where the heroes themselves gathered, and the walls, long high walls crowned with palisades, marvellous to look upon. But when they had come to the splendid palace of the king, the goddess, flashing-eyed Athena, was the first to speak. She said, "Guest, here is the house which you asked me to show you. You will find the kings, cultivated by Zeus, feasting at the banquet. Go inside, and don't be afraid of anything, as a bold person is better in everything, though he is a stranger from another land. First approach the queen in the palace. Her name is Arete, and she comes from the same line as King Alcinous. Nausithous firstly was born from the earth-shaker Poseidon and Periboea, the most beautiful of women, the youngest daughter of great-hearted Eurymedon,[71] who once was king of the arrogant Giants.

Odyssey, 10.80ff.

So for six days we sailed, night and day, and on the seventh day we arrived at the towering citadel of Lamus, at Telepylos of the Laestrygonians, where herdsman calls to herdsman as he drives in his flock, and the other answers as he drives his flock out. There someone who never slept could have earned double wages, one by herding cattle, and the other by pasturing white sheep; for the outgoings of the night and the day are near together.

When we had arrived there at the fine harbor, about which a vertical cliff runs endlessly on both sides, and projecting headlands opposite each other stretch out at the mouth, and the entrance is narrow, then all the others steered in their curved ships. The ships were moored close together in the hollow harbor. There was a bright calm all around, for no waves swelled there, neither small or big. I alone moored my black ship outside, there on the border of the land, securing the cables firmly to the rock. Then I climbed to a great height, to an outlook point, and took my stand there. There was no sign of any cattle or of humans. All we saw was smoke springing up from the land. Then I sent out some of my companions to go and find out the people were, who here ate food on the earth.

I chose two men, and sent a third as a herald along with them. After they had gone ashore, they went along a smooth road along which wagons usually brought wood down to the city from the high mountains. In front of the city they met a young girl drawing water. She was the lovely daughter of Laestrygonian Antiphates, who had come down to the beautifully-flowing spring Artacia. It was from Artacia that they brought water to the town. They approached her and spoke to her, and asked her who the ruler king of these people, and about the people of whom he was master.

She then showed them with the high-roofed house of her father. When they had entered the splendid house, they saw his wife there. She was as huge as a mountain peak. They were horror-stricken at the sight her. She immediately called the magnificent Antiphates, her husband, from the assembly and he planned a horrible destruction for them. He immediately seized one of my companions and was about to eat him, but the other two jumped up and fled to the ships.

Then Antiphates raised a cry throughout the city. When they heard it, the mighty Laestrygonians came crowding from all sides. There were too many of them to count. They were not like humans but were like Giants. They threw rocks as large as a man could lift from the cliffs at us. Immediately am alarming commotion arose throughout the ships, both from men who were dying and from ships that were being crushed. They speared them like fish and carried them home, a detestable meal.

While they were slaying the men within the deep harbor, I drew my sharp sword from beside my thigh, and cut the cables of my dark-prowed ship. I quickly called to my companions to fall to their oars, that we could escape from our evil plight. In fear of death they all tossed the sea with their oar-blades, and set gladly seaward. My ship sped away from the jutting cliffs, but all the other ships were lost there together.

Homer does not mention the Giant War and does not hold to the legend that the Giants had serpent feet or were progeny of Gaia and Ouranos.

Hesiod, *Theogony*, 176-205.

Heaven was happy about his evil doing. However, immense vast Gaia inwardly groaned within, being in difficulties, and she devised a cunning evil plan. She at once made the element of grey flint and shaped a huge sickle, and told her plan to her dear children. She spoke, cheering them on, while her dear heart was grieved: "My children, the progeny of a sinful father, if you will listen to me, we should punish your father's despicable outrage, as he was the one who first thought of doing dishonourable things."

This is what she said, but dread seized them all, and no one spoke. However the great and cunning Kronos took heart and answered his dear mother. "Mother, I will agree to do this deed. I have no respect for our father of evil repute, as he was the one who first thought of doing dishonourable things."

This is what he said. Immense Gaia was exceedingly happy in spirit, and took him and hid him in an ambush, and gave him a jagged sickle, and revealed the whole plot to him. Heaven arrived, bringing on night and longing for love. He lay on top of Gaia, spreading himself out fully on her. Then the son from his ambush stretched forth his left hand and in his right took the great long sickle with jagged teeth, and swiftly lopped off his own father's genitals and threw them away behind him. They did not fall uselessly from his hand, for Gaia received all the bloody drops that gushed forth, and as the seasons moved round she birthed the strong Erinyes and the great Giants with gleaming armor, holding long spears in their hands and the Nymphs who are called Meliae all over the limitless earth.

As soon as he had cut off the genitals with flint and thrown them from the land into the surging sea, they were swept away over the main a long time. White foam spread around them from the immortal flesh, and a young woman grew from it. First she approached sacred Cythera, and after there she went to sea-girt Cyprus, and turned into a frightening and lovely goddess. Grass grew up around her beneath her attractive feet. Both gods and humans call her Aphrodite, the foam-born goddess and richly-crowned Cytherea, because she grew from the foam, and Cythera because she reached Cythera, and Cyprogenes because she was born in billowy Cyprus, and Philomedes because she sprang from genitals. Eros accompanied her, and comely Desire followed her right from her birth and as she went into the assembly of the gods. She has had this honor from the beginning, and this is the portion allotted to her by humans and immortal gods, maidens' whisperings, smiles and wiles with sweet delight, love and kindness.

Chapter 8. Origins of Evil.

The Book of Jubilees 10 says that only one-tenth of evil spirits will be allowed to harm humans.

"'And you know how your Watchers, the fathers of these spirits, acted in my day. And as for these spirits which are living, imprison them and bind them in the place of condemnation, and do not let them bring destruction on the children of your servant, my God, because they are evil, and created in order to destroy. Do not let them rule over the spirits of the living, for you alone can rule over them. Do not let them have power over the just from now on and for evermore.'

"And the Lord our God told us to bind them all. The chief of the spirits, Mastema, came and said, 'Lord, Creator, let some of them stay with me, and let them do as I say, and do everything I tell them to do, because if some of them are not left for me, I will not be able to do what I want with the humans, and they are bent on fraud and being led astray in my judgment, for the wickedness of the humans is immense.' God said, 'Let a tenth of them stay with him, and let the other nine parts descend into the place of condemnation.' He commanded one of us to teach Noah all their medicines, for he knew that they would not behave with integrity or justice. So we did what he said: all the nasty evil ones we bound in the place of condemnation, and we left a tenth of them to be subject to Adversary on the earth. We explained to Noah all the medicines for their diseases, and how they worked, and how to heal them with herbs of the earth. Noah wrote down everything we instructed him about every kind of medicine in a book. Thus the evil spirits were prevented from doing anything to Noah's children."

Adam and the "Fall."

Adam is a word which simply means "human." Genesis 1:27 states, "Elohim created *adam* (the word for the race of human beings) in Elohim's image - Elohim created it in the image of Elohim, Elohim created them male and female." Genesis 5:2 states,

"Elohim created them male and female and blessed them and called them human (*adam*) on the day they were created." The word "Adam" that we see in English translations of Genesis is merely a "transliteration," the result of putting the Hebrew letters into English letters. The translation is "human," person/s of both genders. Hebrew has grammatical gender. Many languages have grammatical gender but English does not. In English, we only use words like "he" and "she" when we are speaking of persons, and we try to find out the biological gender of those persons so we know whether to refer to a particular person as "he" or "she." In languages which have grammatical gender, all nouns, whether or not they refer to persons, have a gender. Hebrew has two genders and Greek has three. These languages use pronouns like "he" and "she" with nouns, such as table, tree, and lake. The pronoun goes with the noun to which it refers.

We need to learn the grammatical gender of the noun to know which pronoun to use. It is exceptionally important to note that grammatical gender does not match biological gender - it may, but by coincidence only. Thus, in ancient Greek, the word for "old woman" is neuter gender. Yet if we were translating a Greek sentence about an old woman into English, we would not refer to the old woman as "it;" we would refer to the old woman as "she". The Greek word for a trench is feminine gender, but in English it would be silly to refer to the trench as "she." We just don't do that in English. English is different from Hebrew and Greek. In Hebrew, the word *adam* is masculine grammatical gender. That means it has to have a masculine pronoun, just as the word for hand (even a man's hand) in Hebrew is feminine and must have a feminine pronoun. Again, this has nothing to do with biological gender. In the account of the *adam* in Genesis, Genesis 1:27 states, "God created human in God's image. In the image of God, God created *oto*." *Oto* is the singular masculine accusative pronoun agreeing with *adam*, the human. It has to be masculine grammatical gender to agree with the gender of the noun. It simply replaces the word *adam*. In English we say "him" because tradition holds that the biological gender of the *adam* was male and the English language does not refer to a person as "it." The verse continues, "Male and female God created *otam*." *Otam* is the plural gender-unmarked accusative pronoun. Grammatically, this refers to the *adam*, humanity. Thus the verse means, "God created humanity in God's image. God created it in God's image, God created them male and female." Thus God did not create the male first, God created the human first, humanity. God did not create a male first and identify humanity with that male's name. The previous verse, 26, states, "Let us make *adam* . . . and let them rule." *Adam* is here treated as a collective noun, agreeing with a plural verb, that is, the human race. Again, the account does not mention a singular male.

Genesis 1:27 speaks of the creation of the *adam*. If the noun is a collective it could either agree with a plural or singular pronoun. That means that we do not know, from the grammar, whether the noun means "human" and thus the first human was androgynous (as the ancient tradition holds), or whether the noun means "humanity".

That is, we do not know whether a single androgynous "human" was created, or whether "humanity", males and females, were created.

Further on, the account consistently refers to males and females under the term *adam*. *Adam* is the general term for humans, both male and female. At the end of chapter 1, all the references to *adam* are in the plural. Genesis 2:5 states that there was no *adam* to cultivate the ground, that humans have not yet been created. The verse makes the point that humans are the only beings on earth that cultivate the soil. There is no reference to maleness in the verse. Genesis 2:7 tells us that God formed the *adam* from dust, breathed into its nostrils the breath of life, and that the *adam* was a living being. We do not know if the noun is collective or singular (as grammatically it could be either), and no gender is specified. Genesis 2:8 says God put the *adam* in the garden. Again, the masculine pronoun is used as it must agree with the grammatical gender, unlike English, where a masculine pronoun would indicate a male person. In verses 16-17, God speaks to the *adam*. At this point, the term *adam* still encompasses male and female.

In Genesis 2:18-19 God says, "It is not good for the *adam* to be alone, I will appoint a suitable helper for it." Again, the masculine personal pronoun in Hebrew simply agrees with the grammatical gender of the Hebrew noun *adam*. It is usually translated as "he" in English, as people have assumed that the *adam* was a male. There is nothing in the grammar to indicate that the *adam* was a male, and animals are first brought as suitable companions. There was no initial idea that a female of the species was lacking. There is no idea, grammatical or otherwise, that the *adam* is a male. In Genesis 2:20, the *adam* gave names to the animals. The *adam* here is now presented in the Hebrew as a singular person, but still there is nothing to suggest that the *adam* was not both male and female. In verse 21, God put a deep sleep on the *adam*, and withdrew the female portion from it. (Hebrew *tsal'ot*, Greek *pleura*, referring to the factor, the portion, it was only later Rabbinic tradition that had "rib".) In verse 22, God shaped that which he had taken from the *adam* into an *isha* (female) and brought her to the *adam*. In verses 23 and 24, the word *isha* (female) is distinguished from the *ish* (male). This is the first time the words for female and male have appeared in the account. The *adam* is now an *ish*, and becomes the individual Adam. However, the meaning of the word *adam* has not changed, he is a human. Yes, he is now, at this point, also a male, but the word *adam* means "human." The female portion was taken out of the human, the *adam*, and became an *isha*. That which was left was still called a human, *adam*. Someone can remove a piece of pie from a whole pie, but the remaining pie is still called a pie. It does not have to be renamed just because a piece of it was removed. The following verse refers to the new two individuals as *ish* and *isha*, male and female. However, Adam as a name does not appear until Chapter 5. This has similar language to chapter 1, where the *adam* is created in God's image, male and female. However, this is followed by a significant statement. After the male and female are introduced, God blessed them, and named them *adam*: "God created them male and female and blessed them and called them human (*adam*) on the day they were created." Thus it is clear that the word *adam* bears no connotations of maleness. When the term is finally applied to the individual male Adam, it is the term *ish* which is used to note his maleness. Thus Adam is now a male, but the word "Adam" does not mean male, it still means "human". The Hebrew word *adam* did not refer to male humans in particular: it means "human," "humanity," and did eventually refer to the husband of Eve, but his name was "Human". Yes, at this point, he was a male human being, but his name was not "Male" in Hebrew, it was "Human."

In *The Assumption of Moses* 11.7 Joshua asks how a human being would dare to bury Moses' body. In the fragments of the lost conclusion, Moses' body is mentioned as the object of a dispute between Michael and the *diabolo* (Latin). The translator R.C. Charles reconstructs the fragments as follows: Michael is commissioned to bury Moses. The adversary opposes the burial on the grounds, firstly, that he is the master of matter so the body should be handed to him.[72]

Michael rebuts, "The Lord rebuke you, for it was god's spirit that created the world and all humanity."

The *diabolo* (Latin) brings the charge of murder against Moses. Michael then charges the *diabolo* with tempting Adam and Eve, not Eve alone.

There is nothing in Genesis to identify the serpent in the Garden of Eden with a chief evil presence "Satan." In fact, Genesis 3:1 says that the serpent was cleverer than all the other animals of the field that God had made. The *Book of Jubilees* 3:28 says that all the animals in the field at that point were able to speak.

Here is the *First Book of Enoch's* account of Gadreel, the one that the *First Book of Enoch* states deceived Eve in the Garden of Eden.[73]

"The name of the first is Jeqon. He was the one who led all the sacred associates of God astray and brought them down to earth, and led them astray with humans. The name of the second is Asbeel. He suggested an evil plan to the sacred associates of God, so that they defiled their bodies with humans. The name of the third is Gadreel. He showed every deadly blow to the humans. He led Eve astray, and showed the humans the weapons of death, the coat of mail, the shield, and the sword for killing, every deadly weapon he showed to the humans. Because of him they have proceeded against the inhabitants of the earth for ever and ever."

Let us look at serpents in the Bible. Job 41 describes the dragon Leviathan as huge, fierce, with scales on its back, states that it breathes fire and smoke, and that arrows and clubs have no effect on it, and that it stirs up the sea when it moves. Job 31 also states that there is no other creature like it on earth. Psalm 71:14 says,

"You crushed the heads of Leviathan." The Ugaritic texts have the dragon with 7 heads defeated by the god Baal and by the goddess Anat.[74] Psalm 71:13 states, "You broke the heads of the dragon in the water." The dragon is named "Rahab" (proud one) in Isaiah 51:9 and Job 26:12. Isaiah 27:1 and Job 26:13 describe the dragon as "squirming." Job 41:19-21 states that the dragon breathed fire and smoke.

The Hebrew Bible / Old Testament does not say that Adam and Eve ate an apple – the identity of the fruit is not mentioned – this is a myth[75] based on John Milton's *Paradise Lost*. In the same way, the snake is not named in the Bible, although *Paradise Lost* does name the snake as "Satan." In the Bible, the snake is not identified with any evil entity but is described as an animal of the field that God had made. Revelation does call the adversary an ancient snake, but this is not evidence that this ancient snake appeared in the Garden of Eden. And even if the two are one and the same, we still do not have the name of the snake.

In 2 Corinthians 11:3, Paul says that "the snake beguiled Eve with his treachery."

In 1 Timothy 2:12-14, Paul says, 12-14 I most certainly do not grant authority to a woman to teach that she is the originator of a man -rather, she is not to cause a fuss - for Adam was formed first, then Eve. And Adam was not deceived, but the woman made a mistake as she was beguiled."

Eve was venerated by the Gnostics as the revealer of knowledge. In 1945 the Nag Hammadi Library, a collection of thirteen ancient codices containing over fifty Gnostic texts, was discovered in upper Egypt. Nag Hammadi texts which include the Genesis creation accounts are: On the Origin of the World, Gospel of Philip, Exegesis on the Soul, Hypostasis of the Archon, Thunder: Perfect Mind, Apocryphon of John, Apocalypse of Adam, and Testimony of Truth. The account in On the Origin of the World is as follows: "After the day of rest Sophia sent her daughter Zoe, being called Eve, as an instructor in order that she might make Adam, who had no soul, arise so that those whom he should engender might become containers of light. When Eve saw her male counterpart prostrate she had pity upon him, and she said, 'Adam!

Become alive! Arise upon the earth!'

Immediately her word became accomplished fact. For Adam, having arisen, suddenly opened his eyes. When he saw her he said, 'You shall be called "Mother of the Living". For it is you who have given me life.'" (*On the Origin of the World* 115:31-35, 116:1-7, The Nag Hammadi Library, ed. James Robinson, rev. ed. San Francisco: Harper, 1988). Eve is also a central figure in *The Hypostasis of the Archons*, and *The Apocalypse of Adam*.

The verses in 1 Timothy 2:13-15 make sense in the light of the threat of Gnosticism as they are a refutation of Gnostic belief. Eve was beguiled (the Greek word suggesting by cunning or supernatural means): Adam was disobedient and sinned. The result was the "Fall."

Before leaving this subject, I will mention the alleged "Antichrist." There is much speculation among some Christian groups as to who the "Antichrist" will be in the end times. However, the Antichrist as an actual sole person is just a myth - the term is not mentioned at all in Revelation, and in fact is mentioned only in 1 John and in 2 John (just once). John uses the term in the plural - he says that anyone who denies that Jesus is the Anointed One is an antichrist (anti-anointing) and says that many antichrists (anti-anointings) have come into the world. At no point does John refer to an "Antichrist" (Anti-anointing) as an individual. There appears to be some confusion among many contemporary Christians who appear to have confused the "Beast" of Revelation with the term "Antichrist". Again, the term "Antichrist" is never used to refer to an individual, and the term appears only here and in 2 John and does not appear in Revelation.

Chapter 9. Was Satan a Fallen Angel?

Revelation 12:7-9 says there was war in heaven and an angel was thrown out with a third of the angels but does not name this angel.
Revelation 12:7-9.
War broke out in heaven. Michael and his Messengers (*angels*) waged war against the dragon, and the dragon and his messengers fought back. But the dragon wasn't strong enough, and thus they no longer had a place in heaven. The mighty dragon was thrown down - that ancient snake called "Slanderer-Liar," and also called "adversary", who leads the whole earth astray. He and his Messengers (*angels*) were hurled to the earth.

This is the account in Isaiah of "Lucifer" (Light-Bearer), equated by modern-day Christians with "Satan."
Isaiah 14:12-21.
"How you are fallen from heaven, Lucifer (Light-Bearer), associate of dawn! How you are cut down to the ground, you who weakened the nations!"
"For you said to yourself, 'I will ascend to heaven and set my throne above El's stars. I will preside on the appointed mountain in the sides of the north. I will climb to above the height of the clouds, I will be like Elyon (*a Hebrew name for God*).'
"But instead, you will be brought down to Sheol, to the sides of the pit. Everyone there will stare at you and ask, 'Is this the one who shook the earth and the kingdoms of the world, that made the world a wilderness and demolished its cities and did not free the prisoners from Sheol?'
"The kings of the nations lie in splendid tombs, but you will be thrown out of your grave like a ritually abominable branch. You will be dumped like the remainder of those slain by the sword with those killed in battle like a corpse trampled underfoot, you will go down to the dungeon. You will not be given a proper burial, because you have destroyed your land and killed your people. The

offspring of evildoers will never be proclaimed. Kill the children of this wrongdoer so they do not rise and conquer the land or rebuild the cities of the world."

However, 1 Enoch names Azazel as the star that fell to earth.
1 Enoch 86:1-6.
Again I looked attentively in my sleep, and surveyed heaven above. And a single star (*Azazel*) fell from heaven! It got up, and ate and grazed among those cows. After that I perceived the large black cows, and all of them changed their stalls and their young cows, and they began to moan one with another!

Again I looked in my vision, and saw heaven, when I saw many stars (*The Watchers*), which descended, and projected themselves from heaven to where the first star (*Azazel*) was! It was the middle of those young cows and cows (*women and men*), grazing among them. I observed them, and they all acted like stallions ready to serve, and began to mount the young cows (*women*), all of whom became pregnant, and gave birth to elephants, camels, and donkeys! (*Giants, Nephilim, and Elioud.*) The cows were alarmed and terrified at this, and began biting with their teeth, devouring, and goring with their horns. And thus they began to eat those cows. All the inhabitants of the earth were terrified, shook with fear at them, and fled away!

Ezekiel 28:11-19.
"The word of Yahweh came to me, 'Human, weep for the king of Tyre and say to him, "Adonai Yahweh says, 'You were full of wisdom and beauty. You were in Eden, Elohim's garden. Your clothing had every precious stone: sardius, chrysolite, diamond, beryl, onyx, jasper, sapphire, and emerald, carbuncle, gold, and the making of the settings was crafted for you on the day you were created.

'You are the anointed cherub that defends. You had access to Elohim's sacred mountain and walked among the fiery stones. You were complete in everything you did from the day you were created until the day injustice was found in you.

'Your great wealth filled you with violence, and you sinned. So I banished you from Elohim's mountain. Mighty guardian, I expelled you from your place among the fiery stones. Your heart was filled with pride because of your beauty. You corrupted your wisdom because of your splendor. So I threw you to the earth and exposed you to the gaze of kings.

'You defiled your sanctuaries with your many wrongdoings and your dishonest trade. So I brought fire from within you, and it consumed you. I will burn you to ashes on the ground in the sight of all who are watching. All who knew you are appalled at your destruction. You have come to a terrible end, and you are no more."

Perhaps the anointed cherub and Lucifer are one and the same, but the Bible does not state this.

Endnotes.

[1] An Aramaic text reads "Watchers," Cf. J.T. Milik, *Aramaic Fragments of Qumran Cave 4*, Oxford, Clarendon Press, 1976, p. 167. Daniel 4:17 mentions a "Watcher." Nebuchadnezzar tells Daniel that he saw in a vision or dream a "sacred Watcher" who appeared to him and made an announcement. In the vision the Watcher concluded, "This announcement is by the decree of the Watchers, this command is by the word of the sacred ones, so that those who are alive may understand that the Supreme has authority over the human kingdoms, and he gives it to whomever he wishes. He sets up even the lowest ranked human beings over them." (From *The Source Bible*.) The *Septuagint* (Greek Old Testament) translates the word for "Watcher" as "angel." However, Theodotion (c. 200 A.D.), the Jewish scholar who made a translation of the Hebrew Bible into Greek, transliterates the word. That is, he simply put it into Greek letters without attempting to translate it, as one does with names.

[2] For the pagan supernatural messenger (pagan "angel") context see inscriptions *ZPE* 30 (1978) 257 n. 7, and *EG* IV.210 (2nd c AD), as well as dedication to pagan *TAM* V, 1.185. The word also occurs in *TAM* V, 1.159 but it is not clear whether the messenger was a human or supernatural messenger. There is evidence for the term occurring in contexts where a derivation from Judaism has been ruled out. There is as yet no conclusive evidence as to whether the famous "Thera angels" were in fact Christian, cf. *IG* XII, 3 (1898) 455, 933-74, *IG* XII, *Suppl.* (1904) 1636, 1637 ($2^{nd} - 3^{rd}$ c. AD).

[3] Jerome, *Letter* 181.4.

[4] See above.

[5] Both the ancient Rabbis and the Church fathers did not acknowledge *bene ha 'elohim* as "associates of God," (properly, "associates of Elohim"). The Rabbis saw them as righteous men and the Church Fathers saw them as Seth's descendants.

Job 2:1

Again there was a day when the associates of God came to present themselves before Yahweh, and Satan also came with them to present himself before Yahweh.

Job 38:7
When the morning stars sang together, and all the associates of God shouted for joy?
Psalm 29:1
A psalm of David.
Assign to Yahweh, you mighty ones (*bene 'elim*),
assign to him splendor and strength!
Psalm 89:7
El is respected in the great assembly of the sacred ones,
he is more awe-inspiring than all who surround him.

[6] Augustine, *City of God*, 15, 23.
[7] See lengthy discussion in J. Massingberd Ford, "'Son of Man' – A Euphemism?" *JBL* 87 (1968), 257-67: Albright, W.F. and Mann, C.S. Matthew: *A New Translation with Introduction and Commentary*, (New York: Doubleday, 1982), pp. CLVI-CLVII, 95; G. Dalman, *The Works of Jesus*, Eng. trans. by D.M. Kay, (Edinburgh, 1902); V. Taylor, *The Gospel According to St. Mark: The Greek text with Introduction, Notes and Indexes*, 1952, London, Macmillan, p. 197.
[8] As there is no extant Hebrew of *The Book of Jasher*, I have used Parry's translation but corrected his idioms and put it into modern English. Parry translates verse 18 thus: "And their judges and rulers went to the daughters of men and took their wives by force from their husbands according to their choice, and the sons of men in those days took from the cattle of the earth, the beasts of the field and the fowls of the air, and taught the mixture of animals of one species with the other, in order therewith to provoke the Lord; and God saw the whole earth and it was corrupt, for all flesh had corrupted its ways upon earth, all men and all animals." J.H. Parry & Company, *The Book of Jasher*, 1887.
[9] R. H. Charles, *The Book of Jubilees*, London, 1902.
[10] CD 16.2.
[11] Likewise the *Book of the Watchers* (1 Enoch 1-36).
[12] Elaine Pagels, *The Origin of Satan: How Christians Demonized Jews, Pagans, and Heretics*, Vintage, 1996, pp. 57-58. The Essenes call Israel's enemy the *kittim*. Pagels sees the *kittim* as a coded

epithet for the Romans and states that they are far more bitter towards their fellow Israelites who "belong to the assembly of Beliar."

[13] Pliny the Elder, *Natural History*, V, XV.
[14] Philo, *Every Good Person is Free*, 75.
[15] Pagels, *op. cit*, p. 57.
[16] *Ibid.*, p 34.
[17] CD 1:13-20.
[18] Pagels, *op. cit*, p. 59.
[19] Josephus, *The Wars of the Jews*, 2.139–142.
[20] A. Cleveland Coxe (Compiler), Alexander Roberts (Editor), James Donaldson (Editor), Philip Schaff (Editor), Henry Wace (Editor) *The Instructions of Commodian*: *Anti-Nicene Fathers* Vol. 4, Hendrickson, 1994, p. 435, vol. 4.
[21] Philo, *On the Giants*, 2:6-7.
[22] Justin Martyr, *Second Apology*, 5.
[23] Here the Greek texts differ from the Ethiopic. One Greek manuscript adds to this section, "And the women bore to the Watchers three races: first, the great Giants who brought forth the Nephilim, and the Nephilim brought forth the Elioud. And they existed and their power and greatness increased."
[24] Or, "and to eat their flesh one after another."
[25] "Herem" was the practice of "sanctification" by total obliteration carried out against certain peoples, such as Jericho, by God's command, around the time of Joshua. See Joshua 6:17-19.
[26] Or, "and to eat their flesh one after another."
[27] That is, angels having sex with human women.
[28] Irenaeus, *Demonstration*, 18. Joseph P. Smith, *St. Irenaeus: Proof of the Apostolic Preaching*, London, 1952, p. 58.
[29] Florentino Garcia Martinez, *The Dead Sea Scrolls Translated*, Leiden, New York, Koln: Brill, 1994, pp. 230–31, 248–50.
[30] Often mistranslated as "giants."
[31] Equally, "ancestors."
[32] The New Testament has Hades as a place separate from heaven, cf. for example, Acts 2:27, 31; Gen. 37:35, 44:29; Job 14:13, 17:13.
[33] Equally possible from the text, "the assembly of El," or "the mighty assembly."

[34] Elohim.
[35] "Light bearer."
[36] Meaning unclear.
[37] Originally Jewish, but preserved today only in Slavonic.
[38] See also *Genesis 15:11*: "Birds of prey came down on the carcasses, and Abram drove them away."
[39] *Apocalypse of Abraham* 13:4-9.
[40] *Apocalypse of Abraham* 31:5.
[41] *Apocalypse of Abraham* 23:7.
[42] *Apocalypse of Abraham* 20:5.
[43] J. Knappert, *Islamic Legends: Histories of the Heroes, Saints and Prophets of Islam* (Leiden: E.J. Brill, 1985), 31-3.
[44] Qur'an, Surah 2:35.
[45] Qur'an, Surah 7:13-19. See also Surah 15:31-48, 17:61-65, 18:50, 20:116-123, 38:71-85.
[46] Abd al-Qadir al-Jilani, *Revelations of the unseen : Futuh al-Ghaib. A collection of seventy-eight discourses*, Abd al-Qadir al-Jilani, translated from the Arabic by Muhtar Holland, Houston, Texas, Al-Baz Publishing, 1992.
[47] Near Damascus.
[48] Most manuscripts here read "not," but scholars such as Charles and Knibbs attribute the "not" to scribal error.
[49] The Ethiopic word is *Ikisat* which means "serpents" and was translated by the Greeks as *drakon*, which means a huge serpent, a python, a dragon. The Hebrew word "Seraphim" can also mean "serpents."
[50] In the Greek, *paradeisis*, commonly transliterated as "paradise," is a Persian loan word meaning a garden of fruit trees (or orchard) which first occurs in Greek in Xenophon's *Anabasis*, 1.2.7. It appears commonly in the papyri and inscriptions in the same meaning. See *I.Tyre* 1.108 (pl.47.1) (late Roman), "I solemnly request those who are going to acquire this orchard...", *P.Petr.* i.16.2.7 (230 B.C.), "the produce of my orchards", *P.Tebt* 1.5.53 (118 B.C.), "the tithes which they used to receive from the holdings and the orchards". *P.Lond* 933.12 (A.D. 211) notes a payment on account of an "olive orchard". See also the Rosetta Stone (*OGIS* 90.15, 196 B.C.). It occurs frequently in the *Septuagint* as a garden, sometimes as the abode of the blessed,

see *Cant.* 5.13, *Eccl.* 2.5, and *Neh.* 2.8. The *Midrash Haggadah* (*Midrash* means a verse-by-verse interpretation of Scripture, and *Haggadah* is an interpretation and expansion of the non-legal portions of Scripture) describes Paradise in detail, as far as giving specific dimensions and furnishings of the chambers. The details are said to have been supplied by individuals who visited Paradise while alive. It states that 9 mortals visited heaven while alive, and that one of these is Enoch. Ezekiel's description of Paradise is similar to that of Enoch's: a great mountain in the middle of the earth which has streams of water flowing from under it. A palm tree grows in the middle of the center of the sacred enclosure. Similar descriptions are to be found in other apocalypses (e.g. *Apoc. Baruch*, 5, *2 Esd.* 8.52). In Rabbinical literature the conception of paradise stands in contradistinction to hell. Paradise is occasionally referred to as "the world to come". The word occurs 3 times in the New Testament: Luke 23:43, 2 Cor. 12:4 and Rev. 2:7.

[51] Nonnus, *Dionysiaca* 36. 241 ff.
[52] Inerant signa expressa, quo modo Titani
bicorpores Gigantes, magnique Atlantes
Runcus ac Purpureus filii Terras. (Gnaeus Naevius, *Bellum Punicum, Fragment.*)
[53] Josephus, *Antiquities of the Jews*, 1.3.1.72ff.
[54] Hesiod, *Theogony* 176, *Bacchylides*, Frag 52. Contra Virgil, *Aeneid* 6.250; Ovid, *Metamorphoses* 4.453; Aeschylus, *Eumenides* 321, *Lycophron* 432, 3.1; Gaius Valerius Flaccus 1.730; Statius, *Thebaid* 12.557 & 11.47; *Orphic Hymns* 29, 70.
[55] Apollonius Rhodius, *Argonautica* 4.1642ff; Hesiod, *Works and Days* 106 ff; Callimachus, *Hymn 1 to Zeus* 42 ff.
[56] Pseudo-Apollodorus, *Bibliotheca* 1. 6.
[57] Nonnus, *Dionysiaca*, 18.237ff.
[58] Diodorus Siculus XIII 81, 1-4.
[59] Pseudo-Apollodorus, *Bibliotheca* 1. 34; Pindar, *Isthmian Ode* 6 Str 2.
[60] Antoninus Liberalis, *Metamorphoses* 21.
[61] Nonnus, *Dionysiaca* 25.85; 48.6.
[62] Pseudo-Hyginus, *Preface*, mentions some Titans in his list of Giants: "From Earth and Tartarus were born Giants: Enceladus, Coeus, Elentes, Mophius, Astraeus, Pelorus, Pallas, Emphytus,

Rhoecus, Ienios, Agrius, Alemone, Ephialtes, Eurytus, Effracordon, Theomises, Theodamas, Otus, Typhon, Polybotes, Meephriarus, Abesus, Colophonus, Iapetus."
[63] Pausanias 8.29.3: "To say the Giants had serpents for feet is absurd."
[64] Stephanus Byzantius, s.v. Phlegra states that Phlegra is said the old name of Pallene.
[65] The Scholiast on Pindar 1.6.32 supports this statement.
[66] "Ally with," "jointly fight with."
[67] The location of the battle of the Olympic gods and Giants was set in different places, cf. Diodorus 5.71; Strabo 5.4.4, 6; 6.3, 5; 7 Fr. 25, 27; 10.5.16; 11.2.10.
[68] The Bacchic wand, the *thyrsus*, which was a wand wreathed with ivy and vine leaves. It had a pine cone on the top.
[69] The helmet or cap of Hades made someone invisible.
[70] A stadion was just over 600 feet (just under 200 metres).
[71] Propertius, *Elegies* 3.9.
[72] R. H. Charles, *The Assumption of Moses: translated from the Latin sixth century ms., the unemended text of which is published herewith, together with the text in its restored and critically emended form.* (1897), London: A. and C. Black.
[73] 69:1-29.
[74] *KTU²* 1.3 3 38-39 and *KTU²* 1.5 I 1-3.
[75] A further myth - the popular belief remains that there were "three" "wise men" and that these people visited Jesus as a baby in a manager. However, the Bible does not mention the number, and in fact states that they visited Jesus in a house. (History tells us that Jesus was around two years of age at the time.) At no time does the Bible, in any translation, suggest or imply that the "wise men" were present soon after Jesus' birth. Further, not one Bible version states the number "three"; this is purely unfounded tradition based perhaps on the number of different types of gifts, not even number of gifts.

You may also be interested in
The Book of Jubilees
By Dr A. Nyland
This is a new (2011) easy-to-read translation and not one of the many century-old public domain translations. *The Book of Jubilees* contains information additional to Genesis and early Exodus, and is the account from creation to the early times of Moses. *The Book of Jubilees* claims to be told to Moses by angels when he was on Mount Sinai. One of the Dead Sea Scrolls, The Damascus Document, states that the Book of Jubilees reveals divine secrets "to which Israel has turned a blind eye." The Essenes, a Jewish sect who lived from the 2nd c. BCE to the 1st c. ACE, coveted *The Book of Jubilees* and kept it in their library. Jubilees are seven "year-weeks," a year-week being a period of seven years, so a jubilee is 49 years.

Book of Enoch: Angels, Watchers and Nephilim
By Dr A. Nyland
The Book of Enoch contains accounts of the Watchers, a class of angel who came to earth and taught humans weapons, alchemy, spell potions, sorcery, astrology, and astronomy. The Watchers also slept with human women and produced the Nephilim. For this, they were punished and cast into Tartarus. This is also mentioned in the New Testament. This is an easy to read translation of *The Book of Enoch* with additional information on angels, Watchers, and Nephilim.

Complete Books of Enoch: 1 Enoch (First Book of Enoch), 2 Enoch (Secrets of Enoch), 3 Enoch (Hebrew Book of Enoch)
By Dr A. Nyland
1 Enoch tells of the Watchers, a class of angel, who taught humans weapons, spell potions, root cuttings, astrology, astronomy, and alchemies. The Watchers also slept with human women and produced the Nephilim. For this, they were imprisoned and cast into Tartarus. This is also mentioned in the New Testament. In 2 Enoch, two angels take Enoch through the 7 heavens. This contains the extended version of 2 Enoch, The Exaltation of Melchizedek. In 3 Enoch, Enoch ascends to heaven and is transformed into the angel Metatron. This is about the Merkabah and is of interest to Kabbalists.

Printed in Great Britain
by Amazon.co.uk, Ltd.,
Marston Gate.